Developing a Security Training Program

Developing a Security Training Program focuses on how to establish a comprehensive training program for a security department from the ground up. This book highlights formal curriculum development, consistent and continual training, and the organizational benefits including how such security training will be a value-add.

It's long overdue for the industry to revisit old security training models from the past – to both general staff as well as to the dedicated security staff and professionals within organizations – and examine and revamp such with a fresh perspective. Given the current, dynamic environment for businesses – and the threats businesses face – it is important that any such training consider all procedures and policies, and be fully integrated into the company culture. This includes maintaining an eye on budgetary and financial costs while recognizing the need to budget for more training resources to maintain resilience and adaptability to current challenges and future changes to the environment. There is only one way to prepare your staff and that is through comprehensive and consistent training.

Developing a Security Training Program provides the blueprint and tools for professionals to provide ongoing, targeted, and comprehensive security training at a low, budget-friendly cost.

Developing a Security Training Program

Joseph McDonald, CPP, PSP, and CPOI

CRC Press
Taylor & Francis Group
Boca Raton London New York

CRC Press is an imprint of the
Taylor & Francis Group, an **informa** business

Front cover image: Wright Studio/Shutterstock

First edition published 2024
by CRC Press
2385 NW Executive Center Drive, Suite 320, Boca Raton FL 33431

and by CRC Press
4 Park Square, Milton Park, Abingdon, Oxon, OX14 4RN

CRC Press is an imprint of Taylor & Francis Group, LLC

Library of Congress Cataloguing-in-Publication Data
Names: McDonald, Joseph (Security expert), author.
Title: Developing a security training program / Joseph McDonald.
Description: Boca Raton : CRC Press, 2024. | Includes bibliographical references and index.
Identifiers: LCCN 2024005023 (print) | LCCN 2024005024 (ebook) | ISBN 9781032274041 (hardback) | ISBN 9781032274034 (paperback) | ISBN 9781003292586 (ebook)
Subjects: LCSH: Private security services--Employees--Training of. | Private security services--United States--Management.
Classification: LCC HV8291.U6 M38 2024 (print) | LCC HV8291.U6 (ebook) | DDC 363.28/9071--dc23/eng/20240408
LC record available at https://lccn.loc.gov/2024005023
LC ebook record available at https://lccn.loc.gov/2024005024

ISBN: 978-1-032-27404-1 (hbk)
ISBN: 978-1-032-27403-4 (pbk)
ISBN: 978-1-003-29258-6 (ebk)

DOI: 10.4324/9781003292586

Typeset in Palatino
by MPS Limited, Dehradun

CONTENTS

SECTION I Developing Any Coursework

SECTION II Layered and Secondary Course Development

ABOUT THE AUTHOR

Joseph H. McDonald, CPP, PSP, CMAS, CPOI, is a retired Chief Security Officer (CSO) for Switch Ltd., where he was responsible for building the technology and data center company's personnel, physical, critical infrastructure, and information security auditing for certifications (HIPAA, PCI, SSAE, ISO 2700X, FISMA, etc.). For the past 35 years, McDonald has worked in many aspects of the security profession, as a private investigator, police officer, corporate facility security officer (FSO) for a defense contractor, security director for a national bank, senior security consultant, and an engineered systems sales manager for major systems integrators, where he designed large security and surveillance systems. Combining his education and experience in curriculum development, McDonald combined security and training to produce a complex training program for a large security department. McDonald has served as secretary, treasurer, and vice president of the ASIS Board of Trustees for the organization's international foundation. In addition, he spent two terms on the ASIS Board of Directors and four years as council vice president, where his leadership and oversight guided six councils and their volunteer members. McDonald is often sought for his opinions on training, certification programs, procedures, and policy issues, and he was appointed to The International Foundation for Protection Officers Board of Directors and currently is a member of the IFPO Advisory Board.

FOREWORD

Security is an illusion.

A simple yet thought-provoking quote, scribbled hastily in the margin as I interviewed the Chief Security Officer for a global technology company, well over two decades ago, these four simple words are highlighted in my published dissertation research (2009) on violence. Since that time, countless training sessions have commenced with this same opening quotation (including appropriate credit, of course) sparking provocative discussion among the participants. The citation notes "Joseph McDonald" and truer words were never spoken.

Dear reader, you are here because you already know there is much more than the stereotypical "guns, guards, and gates" to this profession. Misunderstood and often under-rated by society, security is critical and constantly changing to meet evolving threats. An amalgamation of numerous overlapping disciplines, to truly reflect society requires constant learning and adaptation. While the guns, gates, and guards are equally important and visible, less obvious areas that cannot be over-emphasized include background screening, making personnel decisions, communication skills, critical thinking, strategic thinking, and so on to name a few; and ongoing training, training, and more training.

For those of us who choose this career path as a life-long pursuit, we typically find our way by default, and seldom by design. Joe is an exception. Readers will benefit from relevant examples shared throughout the book drawn from Joe's extraordinary career including military service (always) as a Marine, serving as a law enforcement officer, and as the Chief Security Officer who helped build a world-renowned global technology company.

Joe brings a combination of formal education, including expertise in adult learning, too many professional credentials to name, extensive training, and expertise; there is no substitute for "been-there-done-that-fixed-it" experience. He is truly a lifelong learner and the epitome of scholar–practitioner–leader–teacher; his pursuit for perfection (if such a thing exists) in the art and science of security shines through in the subsequent pages. I think this is his way of paying it forward; leaving a lasting legacy to security, and I am awestruck by the results.

Joe is always "thinking out of the box" and brings the voice of reason to oftentimes challenging discussions. His imposing stature and baritone voice commands a room. Despite the gruff façade (to some), he and together with his wife are the most compassionate, caring, and generous people on the planet. From supporting K-9 programs for local underfunded law enforcement to spearheading grass-roots collection drives for the annual Toys-4-Tots campaign and ensuring their family members receive an education; they are always putting others first and taking care of family and their community. Why is it important to know this about the author? Because Joe is absolutely *passionate* about training, and it comes through in his words.

I have had the privilege to work with Joe over the years in a volunteer leadership capacity at the local, national, and international levels. The capstone of these experiences was in 2018; together with a small group from the Las Vegas area, we were honored to host the Secretary of the Department of Homeland Security, Kirstjen Nielsen, to showcase an innovative school security improvement program in collaboration with the ASIS Foundation Board of Trustees. This is yet but one example of Joe's dedication to our profession and society.

There are many books about training that address the basics of lesson plans and presentation skills. However, I challenge the reader to find another work that artfully addresses the needs and unique challenges of security by a recognized expert in the field.

This work is destined to become the cornerstone of your professional library that will endure for decades to come.

The following pages will challenge you – enjoy the journey.
Linda Florence, Ph.D., CPP

Security is mostly a superstition. Life is either a daring adventure or nothing.

–Helen Keller

PREFACE

Security training is not a luxury nor a single event; rather, it should be viewed as an ongoing process of investigation and continuous improvement to adjust and respond to threats in the ever-changing landscape.

Linda Florence, Ph.D., CPP
*Former President, International Foundation
of Protection Officers*

I have been responsible for the development and training of both technical and tactical critical tasks with multiple organizations. Based on these experiences, I have penned this book to ensure that regardless of where your organizational training projects currently reside, you will be able to identify the correct components to turn multiple stand-alone or singular training events into a comprehensive curriculum that fits your organizational needs and goals. This book also covers the efforts necessary to set up a security training program for your organization. Whether your organization is just starting its training efforts or has a comprehensive training curriculum but needs documentation for organizational structure, this book will assist your staff's development efforts.

The book discusses the motivations to train, setting up a budget for requesting money, time, and resources, and the documentation and research to ensure well-developed courseware. The discussion will continue with identifying what topics need to be included in your training and the research required to ensure what you are teaching is correct, necessary, and relevant. The first section will discuss the components of courseware, including a lesson topic guide, student guide, instructor guides, student and course evaluations, and tests, to name a few.

This section includes the need to sell the training program to whomever you are required to gain approval. This approval will consist of obtaining funds, personnel, space, and equipment for providing a safe and quality training program. Selling the training program may not be appealing to you; however, you must know that the more your management position is elevated, the requirement to sell your ideas and processes, and requesting budgetary line items will become a significant part of your job description. The writing will give you rational reasons why training is vital to your success and the success of your entire department.

The section then delves into the research and documentation necessary to ensure the training fits the needs of your organization and department. It will also identify how the carefully developed task analysis, training plans, curriculum, and records of training will assist as evidence for audits and, in some cases, litigious actions.

The book's second section will discuss baseline or new hire training for security personnel, and additional methods to enhance your baseline security training. These suggested training vehicles will provide your department with ideas for the continuous and ongoing training that is important in the career development of your staff, the professionalism of your department, assuring you maintain a well-trained operational security team, the introduction of new processes, changing the environment, reminding of the position's primary roles, and remedying flaws and mistakes found during audits or events.

The most important use of these additional training events is to confront change and to promote the ever-evolving and robust nature of the security profession and your industry. Think of the training you have received in the past: was it fulfilling, educational, needed, or just dull and seemingly a waste of your time with a smattering of essential insights? The training options discussed in the sections below will give opportunities to change that mindset from wasteful to performance-enhancing.

I hope you find this book helpful and assisting in your successful training programs.

ACKNOWLEDGMENTS

I would like to thank and dedicate this book to all in the security industry, including everyone I have ever worked with in that industry. From standing post, running a security operations center, developing work schedules, being a volunteer leader for several professional associations in the industry, and managing the operations of multi-site security operations which included a sub-department for the training of personnel. I have enjoyed being a part of the organizations large and small, and most importantly, the people who worked with me to increase the effectiveness and professionalism in these efforts.

From protecting my country as a Marine, protecting and enforcing the law as a police officer, and for the many companies I have assisted in their protection, I may not have known it at the time, but protection as a service to others, in one flavor or another, seems to be my credo. There is no better person to sell an idea through training than a person who believes in the products and matters of which they act, speak, and do. There is truly a necessity to prepare future generations of security personnel – it cannot just be left to chance. The current roles performed by security may not seem critical to the masses or even to the myriad of tasks required for any organization's daily operations, but a security post not manned, or granting access to the wrong person to a protected area is all that it can take to cause a critical event. Believe in what you do, research and draft ethical practices, followed by documenting, and providing the time, resources, and effort necessary to train staff to perform in a professional and cognizant manner. These are our responsibilities.

I would be remiss in not thanking my wife for her patience, understanding, and love.

LEGAL DISCLAIMER

This text is not a legal document and therefore should not be leaned on for any legal aspects of developing specific training materials. Definitions of terms related to law are merely an example. With the multiplicity of countries, states, and municipalities, and the rapid changes to their laws, this text does not attempt to keep up with the various state laws on how the various forms of security are determined, or their requirements throughout the state and federal laws.

As stated throughout the text, research as to how your organization is viewed by local and larger governments is a primary responsibility during the task analysis phase of course development.

Introduction

Like many in our profession, we come from varied backgrounds. Our culture, history, geographic locations, and experiences, good and bad, make us what we are and who we are. They enhance our worth and provide our staff and employer with a more profound sense and global view of the risks associated with the performance of your team and the operation of the security department. My adult education background includes a trade school, a police academy, and undergraduate and graduate degrees. My professional background includes military service (USMC), municipal law enforcement, and many aspects of security, including system design, investigations, consulting, and management, from Security Manager to Chief Security Officer of a publicly traded corporation.

During my military service, I first encountered curriculum development as I had my initial experiences of providing classroom and practical technical training exercises followed by an emphasis on developing coursework. After four years in attack and observation aircraft squadrons, I spent another four years as a technical instructor. During these four years, I taught in formal military classrooms and conducted hands-on practical technical exercises to remove, maintain, and install complicated and technical aircraft components. During a typical lab exercise, students were required to completely disassemble, inspect, reassemble, install, and calibrate systems such as the gun turret of the Cobra helicopter.

I was also responsible for assisting in the upkeep of the courseware I taught. These upkeep tasks included developing new courseware for multiple subjects, updating existing wares, and recertifying the validity and necessity of the courses with subject matter experts in the field. When validating courses offered, I conducted task analysis interviews and workshops with active combat-ready personnel to correct, verify, and validate that the highly technical skills of wherein my organization trained future service personnel were useful, correct, and necessary for those graduates before being assigned combat roles.

I was honored to receive the Navy's certification and title of Master Training Specialist. With that title, I was granted the extra task of being a primary author of a collection of specific courses. This extra responsibility

DOI: 10.4324/9781003292586-1

included project management in the workflow processes and meeting preset timetables and deadlines. These tasks required a great deal of editing for quality assurance of the courseware and required documentation to ensure the deadlines were met.

During my career in law enforcement, I was assigned as a tactical officer (TAC) at several police academies where my responsibilities fell to classroom and field exercise management techniques in a semi-stress environment. I was certified to teach several Police Officer Standard of Training (POST) courses and the training of coworkers and subordinates as I rose through the ranks.

I was fortunate to be hired to teach at a post-secondary security officer school where I was tasked with methodically documenting the curriculum produced at the school for publication and state certification. In this role, I was introduced to state regulatory requirements regarding security officers, security training, and certification in the powers to arrest, baton, firearms, and teargas.

At the request of a community college's Criminal Justice Department head, I developed introductory courseware for Occupational Safety and Health (OSHA) for security professionals. The course was presented and accepted by the college system and added to their course offerings. Again, the critical aspect of this effort for me was the research and working within the requirements to obtain approval for the coursework within a community college system.

After leaving law enforcement and transitioning to various security positions, I presented at many international security seminars and conferences, was selected as a keynote speaker at conferences and company sales meets, and consulted with customers to assist in developing policies and procedures that documented the proper use of their physical security systems within their organizational needs and current practices. This was when I came to recognize how profoundly important training with standardized course objectives for security staff enhance productivity, regiment the use and deployment of technology and policies, and increase awareness of risks.

I am a member of several security professional associations. Of these, I served in various leadership positions with ASIS International, ASIS Foundation, and the International Foundation for Protection Officers (IFPO) leading to Board of Director positions for these. With these associations and others, I support professional certifications and hold a lifetime Certified Protection Professional (CPP) and lifetime Physical Security Professional (PSP) from ASIS International, a Certified Master Antiterrorism Specialist (CMAS) from the Antiterrorism Advisory Board (ATAB), and a Certified Protection Officer Instructor (CPOI) from the IFPO.

Regardless of the position in which I was employed, the need to develop policies, procedures, practices, and courseware to implement security protocols within my department and the entire organization was the most relevant and demanding of acquired management skills. These skills included listening to stakeholders, drafting and editing documents, selling the need, tone, and verbiage of the document, and delivering the written communication to staff and customers.

Most recently and lastly, my position required that I initiate and oversee the development of a training group within the security operations, and the development of a complete curriculum. For security personnel, courseware included security academies, fire-fighting, first aid/CPR (Cardiopulmonary Resussitation)/automatic electronic defibrillator (AED), certification in handcuffing, self-defense, use of weapons, active shooter tactical deployment, a formal on-the-job training curriculum, and associated courses for customers, vendors, and employees in multiple states, cultures, and countries.

NOTE:
Security has long been a para-military profession where admittedly similar qualities fit many security needs. This writing does not promote the need for your department to mirror a military or law enforcement organization. However, military and law enforcement are critical infrastructures where their personnel is placed in life-threatening situations requiring training at a level unrecognized by most academic or technical environments in criticality and specification. The training methodologies developed and used by law enforcement and military branches require that they ensure the critical training is comprehensively understood and put to use having confirmed that there has been adequate development of excellent and consistent training tactics and practical examples that work extremely well in all levels of stress. Therefore, this writing will point to those training practices that can be tailored to work within your training department and which may be currently in place by law enforcement and military groups, such as an academy, field training program, and tactical decision games. Your organization may not require a high-stress training environment likened to military boot camps or police academies. However, your needs in semi-stress situations may require an elevated training environment to ensure a functional staff under duress.

3

Section I

Developing Any Coursework

1

Selling Your Training Needs and Efforts

INTRODUCTION

Before discussing the development of training programs for your security department, there is an important factor that will be required of you throughout this process. That factor is selling your Security Department's training ambitions and needs while enumerating the benefits of a well-designed and presented curriculum. You will need to constantly sell these ideas as you request money, hours, space, equipment, and personnel to conduct your organization's necessary and requisite training. The selling will not end there, you will need to market the requirement and importance of the training to your staff, your instructors, and leadership. Training is too critical to take for granted by anyone within the training spectrum.

There are several successful approaches to assist you in promoting your training program, but I find that one of the most useful is: "Selling by Example." Who you are, and why you were selected and hired for this position is a good starting point in selling a full training program. You attended countless hours of in-person training events and online courses, sat through many conferences, and read stacks of periodicals and books on your profession. You attained certifications in management and other applicable specific aspects of your position. You have an academic degree. You have years of speaking at conferences, providing training to others for their attainment of professional certification, reviewing

DOI: 10.4324/9781003292586-3

courseware, and a plethora of other experiences. You were put in this position to manage and lead your security department professionally and systemically which you cannot do adequately without time, assets, and money to train the personnel.

Do you believe in the benefits of a strong training program? If you do, you can sell the idea and ask for what you need to put into the training. Believing in the process and professing your willingness and want to put forth the effort is critical to the positive selling of the idea.

Many training requirements come from the mistakes that put your department on notice by upper management. Most security professionals whom I have spoken to always reflect on mistakes by their staff as a reason why training is critical or why ensuring that the topics trained are understood and put to use.

- What did we do that caused the mistake?
- Was enough training provided?
- Was any training provided?
- Did we do a good job of expressing how we wanted the task performed?
- Could training have precluded the mistake?
- Was there a comprehension check after the training?
- Was the mistake a matter of training or comprehension and retention of the topic?

These questions depict your engagement and responsibility to the management and leadership of your staff. Anytime one of your subordinates makes a mistake, it is your mistake to own. If it was combat and not "just" security, would you have been satisfied with the amount of training provided or the fervor, import, and effort put forth in the training? Are you satisfied with the amount of training currently being provided to your staff?

Start at the beginning. The first review of your training plan should be the legal requirements to provide security training. Reviewing requirements is a good starting point and is unquestionably responsible. Research the profession, and local, state, and federal statutes so that you fully understand the necessary course topics of your security training.

The regulations requiring security training topics should be looked at as your minimum training requirements. This includes if the statutes apply to your organization. If your security officers are not required to attend general security coursework put on by the municipality, ensuring your training covers these same topics is recommended as these are minimum requirements. Not the complete course but start with the minimums as a basis for training. Our profession has had its share of hard realities when it comes to training, in that training has a price that most departments do not budget. And that after an event, all training is lacking in some form.

If the state in which your organization works requires that contract security officers be trained in topics X, Y, and Z, then your security officers, though they may not be required to take the state training as they may be a proprietary force, should be trained in topics X, Y, and Z.

Now take a step beyond the minimums required by the statutes and review what your peers provide in training regarding those regulations. What additional training topics do they require of their security personnel, and determine the rationale for their efforts? This may be harder to do than expected. Many in our profession do not have formal training and therefore may not have a curriculum for you to review. There may also be a requirement by their company to not share the training they provide in fear that it may open them to risk.

Should you come to one of these issues, here are a few tactics to get what you need:

- Ask for broad topics only – no specifics.
- Be willing to sign a nondisclosure statement. The intent is to determine what topics you need to train, not to compete or attest in a civil or criminal case regarding their training.
- Talk to the security director regarding the training and the amount of time allotted for training and topics.
- Be willing to reciprocate with a copy of your training topics commensurate with the level of detail provided to your organization.

Security and security training is a process that is hard to sell when there appear to be no problems, no crime, no loss, and no risk. But then, your security doctrine may be what created an environment in which nothing significant occurred. Unfortunately, lacking visible problems may require additional documentation to sell the need for a robust training department. Having answers for this possibility in advance will assist in selling your idea of a complete training plan.

- The growth and future direction of your organization will enable your staff to be able to deal with potential risks through security training.

- Show what your staff does daily that allows for the prevention of problems and where training can assist your staff to be more efficient.
- Organizations want security to be more of a customer service department and production multiplier than the standard security operation. Offer training to your staff toward an approach to serve both internal and external customers.
- With positive notes, list negative events that have occurred at nearby organizations or companies that provide similar services in similar industries. List the event, how it would be mitigated by your staff, and how providing additional training can substantially negate future such events.

A word of caution: sales through fear or intimidation are sometimes effective but are typically short-lived. Use positive examples of why training is critical to your operation rather than using fear tactics. Let those from whom you seek budgetary numbers and personnel identify the consequences of your staff not receiving training.

WHY TRAIN

Several reasons to provide training to your staff are discussed next. You may need for staff to perform a task the same way each time, a new policy may need to be introduced and explained, professional development sets your internal leads apart from each other, and allowing them to excel helps your department and the organization. Utilize the following reasons for why you want to train your staff in your approach to request assets to fulfill your training needs.

Personal Reasons

Training is an expression of self and self-growth. When reading any periodical, watching a video blog, attending a webinar, or taking academic coursework you are learning, and whether realized or not, combining the newly digested material along with your experiences and past knowledge creates the ability to self-train. A key factor here is that the subject of the magazine article, webinar, and class does not matter. You take in all the information and assimilate, discard, consider, and file the information with other information, combine that new information with existing knowledge, and then consider that new information to modify and add to your experience and skillsets to find usage in your personal life, your position, and your self-worth. Continuous self-education is a true hallmark of the professional.

Selling the idea of training yourself is critically important. You do not know everything there is to know about your profession, management, organization, science, the arts, language, grammar, vocabulary of other topics, current events, and so on. Therefore, you need to renew your life-long education. You will never know too much and your vast breadth and knowledge scope with a specific focus on your profession will assist you in making decisions, in the speed of decisions, in seeing the bigger picture, learning about yourself, learning about your subordinates, and how their strengths can be used to better the organization.

Here are a few more reasons why you should continue your training:

- You need to keep up with your profession and craft. Security is an ever-changing profession that ebbs and flows with current worldly events that affect the community and industry. How do new protective technologies work? Where will they fill a need in your operations? Would your organization benefit from additional or enhanced security modeling: enterprise security risk management (ESRM), intelligence, crime prevention through environmental design (CPTED), internal threat monitoring, investigation protocols, certifications, and so on? How can you know the answers to these questions if you are not versed, or at least familiar with these security doctrines?

- You need to educate yourself about the industry in which your organization performs. An in-depth knowledge of your organization's operations and its security risks and concerns is vital to ensure your continued employment and that the courseware you are developing is replete with the needs of your operations. What does your organization do, where do they fit into the community or similar and competing organizations, and what is the meaning of terms used by your company, are these terms cultural or technical? What information about your organization do you not understand: accounting, corporate structure, human resources, operations, engineering, building maintenance, and so on? Learn so you are more valuable to the organization's management team with the ability to identify risks based on your organization's industry.

- You need to be ready for change. Companies purchase other companies, organizations merge, and contracts come to an end. Business changes of these sorts cause drastic upheaval that may affect your status within the organization – both positive and negative changes. Are you ready to take your boss's position? Are you ready to oversee the security of three additional divisions, 900 acres of oil fields, 200 additional security professionals, and so on? Are you ready to look for another job? As change is the only constant in life, embracing the persistence of change is a great quality for leaders, managers, and administrators.
- You need flexibility. The big changes are one thing, but what of the policy additions, pandemics, labor disputes, unhappy employees, and ethical problems in one of your locations? Your continuous education can keep you flexible and prepared for life's little stressors and give you the ability to handle them professionally and rapidly. You may never have enough experience with these issues but your awareness gives you a successful edge toward a strategic direction for seeking solutions and answers.
- Your self-training regimen should be viewed by your subordinates as the norm. Training is too often looked upon in a negative light. Maybe it is that prior training events were a waste of time, the instructor was boring or did not know the material, the training room was too cold, and the seats were too hard. Regardless of the reason, training needs to be set on a pillar as beneficial and worthwhile.
- Training can cause scheduling issues in the daily schedule. You should find that if your subordinates know that you continuously self-educate and the idea of training attendance is a positive within your department, then they will be more accepting of attending and delivering training events, and maybe being selected for training will be seen as a perk for doing a good job or steps toward promotion.

Ultimately, everyone must take responsibility for professionalizing themselves, there is no excuse for not doing so, it needs to be a lifetime commitment, and when done well generates advantages beyond those acquired from the immediate skills and knowledge acquired. For example, training provides an opportunity to network, make friends, build alliances, identify talent and so much more. We enrich ourselves and set an example for others. Come on, time to register for the next course now.

Professor Martin Gill
Director of Perpetuity Research and Founder of the
Outstanding Security Performance Awards (OSPAs)

Personnel

Why should you train your staff? In a well-defined organization, this is a question that should not need to be answered. But as it is the basis for selling your training needs, here are a few points to consider.

Training personnel is the solemn duty of every person responsible for subordinates and team members. The military requires that every person of a higher rank or position train their subordinates to perform to the highest possible operational level with the mindset that when change comes, such as a transfer, promotion, or loss on the battlefield, the subordinate can not only continue doing their job well but can replace the leader. Hopefully, your security work is not so hostile; however, the mantra holds. Your staff and their performance are a reflection of you and your performance. The only way to keep your staff's performance in a manner that your organization ascribes is through the training cycle: train, evaluate, and correct.

A few reasons to train that should easily respond to this question are as follows:

- The obvious reason is to train them to do their job. Security is not an inherent trait. Can anyone stand at a closed gate? Yes. But can they perform with tact, bearing, and the acumen that you prescribe without training? And, is that the sole duty of the position for which you are hiring? Your staff needs to know their job. The idea of security is quite basic to some, but recent research proved the contrary. Staff may have passed the minimal requirements of a basic course and received approval through background checks and minimum requirements to work the post but when sent to another post or filling a new role, a new level of training is required for three reasons:
  - Knowing the job,
  - Capable of performing at a level that is deemed necessary, and
  - Performing with a greater level of confidence.

13

- Training is required. In most jurisdictions, the laws require minimum training for security officers. If your organization falls within these requirements, then ensure those needs are met. If your organization falls outside the jurisdictional purview, then the basic training your organization provides its security force should mimic what is required by the jurisdiction. Other training requirements may be dictated by contractual obligations, laws regarding the carrying of weapons, powers to arrest, and requirements to meet certain industry certifications. This book does not subscribe to providing only the minimal training required, but as a basis for the need to train, "it is required by law" cannot be under-stressed.
- When all your staff have entered their position with the same training baseline, they become a member of the team. Team building allows for flexibility in roles, gives excitement and competition to the roles, and even when a post is boring or stressful, the team knowledge promotes an understanding of quality and ensures adequate comprehensive coverage.
- The continuous training that builds on prior training gives proof of a future in the profession and within the organization. If your staff knows that they are being trained or groomed for future roles, it promotes job satisfaction, job excitement, and job efficiency.
- If we consider security as a paramilitary role, then being mission-oriented gives cause and motivation to employees. Knowing that the taskings are more than a job description gives greater meaning to the task.
- Staff retention. Turnover in the security entry-level vocation is generally high. One way of keeping your staff is to ensure that they know their job well, they see appreciation by the organization through training efforts, and they can foresee a potential elevated position and promotion through obtaining more training. Training your staff is a motivator to keep and retain quality personnel who know their job, perform at high levels, and see a permanent place for themselves in the organization.

An organization's commitment to training and development must be a cornerstone of the culture and included in the . business strategy to ensure long-term growth and success.

Linda Florence, Ph.D., CPP
*Former President of the International
Foundation of Protection Officers*

Organization

I would hope that the person to whom you report hired you to not only do your job but to continuously grow the position, department, and security posture of the organization through updated current practices, a flexible organization, professional associations, networking, and all within the legal boundaries that your organization operates. Not all employers can articulate this point, but when reminded of your numerous progressive roles, the acceptance can be quickly noted.

The benefits of training your staff for the organization may be the greatest benefit to a robust and well-developed training program. Here are a few reasons that your organization will want to have a security department training program:

- Risk avoidance is the name of the security game. It is the reason for most security roles within any organization. If the security component is not trained, and not trained well, that fact increases the risk instead of reducing risk. It is hard to watch any news program without seeing the inappropriate actions of an organization's employees being headlined. Remember, it is not just someone performing badly, it is the fact that the person works for an organization, and their performance is quickly ascribed as how that organization performs all its jobs, produces products, and has a place in society. Training reduces the potential for bad actions and bad reactions. Marrying continuous training with constant supervision enhances that reduction. One of the key elements of a due diligence review is to observe the actions of security staff and review training records. No training, poor training records, or a lack of good training is considered negatively during such a review.
- A trained staff is more cost-effective. Standardization of tasks allows staff and customers to know what to expect of your procedures and the speed and efficiency with which they can perform their jobs. Slowness at a gate or not checking a door to confirm it is secure costs time and is a potential loss to the organization.
- A trained staff is more efficient. Efficiency increases customer satisfaction and saves money. Being a frequent traveler, I hear the complaints as passengers go through security to enter the airside security zone. The frequent complaints are about slow, untrained, or short-staffed positions. The level of security is not

in question, but the speed and efficiency of the staff to perform their tasks is the constant complaint. What about your organization, is security seen as an impediment to operations? Does your security allow customers or employees through a portal with efficiency and speed while still providing good security? Is any delay created by a security operation considered by your organization to be justified? Security is a balance between protection, efficiency, and irritation.

- Your organization has its way of doing things. Training the security staff in the "company way" promotes the ideals and beliefs of the organization as a whole. Initiating staff in the culture of the company is valuable to maintaining the ethical standards, mission statement, company goals, and strategic direction of the organization.
- Every organization hopes to have a group of departments performing in an orchestrated fashion that promotes efficiency and the company vision. Ensuring the whole staff is trained to function within the organization is optimal for efficiency and cost savings. Security is sometimes seen as an operational inhibitor. A door that sticks, a slow card reader, or a process that has not been updated to newly adopted operational activities degrades efficiency. Therefore, training as a means of selling the new security activity, process, or technology with a mind toward inclusivity of all staff is vital to minimizing delays and increasing efficiency while maintaining a high level of security.
- A motivated and well-trained security department allows for confidence at the executive level. If key stakeholders concern themselves with the behavior of a single security staff member or the whole department, it is an unnecessary distraction for both the stakeholder and you. Take away your executives' stressors by having a well-trained and supervised security staff.
- Security as a sales tool is a follow-on to the item above. When was the last time security had anything to do with sales? What if your department is known for its professionalism, customer service, training, certifications, education level, pay scale, and bearing? Does your department provide a noteworthy secure environment for its employees and customers? Be a security force that provides an environment where customers want to be.
- Here is one for Human Resources – a trained staff, a staff that expects continuous training and education has less turnover.

Think of how much time you will save not being involved with disciplinary issues, or looking for new candidates.

From the operational level to the C-Suites, we all perform a vital role in safeguarding our company's critical assets; And a well-trained and security-conscious workforce helps an organization gain a competitive advantage.

Richard Chase, CPP, PSP, PCI
Past President of ASIS International and
government/private sector CSO

Legal

At some point in your career, the actions of your subordinates or team members will come into question. Whether the question comes from an employee, customer, executive, or other parties you owe it to yourself, the company, your profession, and subordinates to be able to prove the validity of the training delivered, training received, and training competency and knowledge retention through documentation and references.

You will need to prove that the training administered was well-researched, fully documented, and professionally delivered. And that the student understood the material and at the time of the training could use the training successfully. Therefore, if the training is poor in any of the above attributes, then retraining is necessary and should be done at a cyclic rate as identified through your research.

- Marksmanship is a diminishing skill that requires constant practice. The hand–eye coordination of safely drawing the weapon, aim point, and breathing control all the while thinking of what is beyond the target and the employee's safety requires constant and regular retraining and practice. This and other subjects need to be researched as to the frequency of training.
- Here are two cases that brought to the court's attention the training received by security officers.

Case Law Regarding Negligent Training and Supervision
In several cases where negligent training and supervision were charged in civil matters, it was found

that the court concludes that the standards of police and security training relate to an occupation that is "beyond the ken of the average layman." A jury evaluating this count of negligent supervision, having only the facts and arguments submitted by the plaintiffs in front of them, would be forced to engage in "idle speculation" regarding the duty of care governing [the company] the training of their employees, and such speculation on the part of a jury is not permissible.

Joes v. Safeway Stores, Inc., 314A.2d 459, 460–461 (C. 1974), and *Parker v. Grand Hyatt Hotel*, 124F. Supp. 2d 79 – Distr. Court, Dist of Columbia 2000

In these cases, the plaintiff needed to bring before the court testimony from a specialized witness who could attest that the training received was negligent.

Case Law Regarding Failure to Train

In this specific case, the plaintiff was tased in a hospital after suffering from morphine delirium. The plaintiff brought forth that the training provided was for "basic security" and "in-house Taser training," but stated that it "does not describe or delineate the constitutional limits of the use of force." And that security guards "were never trained in the constitutional limits of the use of force." The allegations point out a "specific deficiency" in training rather than "general laxness or ineffectiveness in training."

Anthony Smith v. Centra Health, Inc. et al, Case No. 6:20-cv-00016 U.S. District Court, W.D. Virginia, 2021

This case has not been settled yet. This in itself is an issue that security training departments need to understand the length of time that training records need to be kept and available.

The Profession

The security profession is not always seen in the public's best light. Security is too often seen as telling people what they cannot do, rather than providing a secure environment. Though people in our profession save lives, protect the untold value of assets, and perform professionally every hour of every day, the general public does not always see security as having great value. Poorly trained and equipped personnel harm our professional reputation. Untrained and improperly hired personnel cause problems for the public and your organization. The only way to better the public personification of security officers is to provide the adequate and professional training required to perform the job. Train the staff often and consistently with those skills required for the position. And, it is your job to better the security profession through training yourself, your staff, and your organization.

- Your staff is the future of the profession. Every course they attend prepares them for the day they take over as a site supervisor, crisis manager, or take up other management roles. Ensuring your staff receives the necessary and enhanced training courses will prepare them for success and the success of our profession.
- Several security-related professional associations around the world have spent considerable funds and time developing certification programs and certificate programs within the varied security professions. Many of these certifications have been successfully accepted in the security profession and are having favorable results in the industry. Considering that associations promote your profession and offer compounding training, libraries, and benefits to its membership and the profession as a whole, these certifications should be goals for yourself and your staff. It is rewarding to see a fellow security professional attain certification and proudly sign their name with well-earned trailing initials.
- Promoting your profession includes promoting the efforts of your fellow security professionals and your staff who work toward certification, attend training events, and perform in an exemplary fashion. For the profession, we need better press, better acclaim for our efforts, and acceptance as a profession. Your training course development does these things.
- The history of security is not always pretty or spectacular. There are those organizations that understand the necessity of security but for several reasons, they do not put forth the effort, budget, or management toward the effort. As a security professional, you are aware that pointing to a person in uniform standing at a post is not in itself security. Unfortunately, in some venues, this is what may be found. I have asked security personnel for assistance in directions to a venue to be told "I don't know" or "ask another." I have witnessed poorly dressed, poorly postured, and poorly trained security personnel. Yes, I blame the person to whom I witness, but I also question the professionalism of the organization that placed that officer in public to perform a task as a part of security operations.

- With a history of hiring the poor and uneducated, the profession or vocation of security has developed itself into a better class of employees over the decades. Starting with the hiring practices, background investigations, and training requirements, our profession has seen advancements in identifying risks and putting forth practices to mitigate those. Organizations around the world have worked hard to break the old security officer stereotypes and promote the ideals of a professional security workforce. Academic coursework, graduate degrees, professional certifications in general, and those of specific security functions, and licensing requirements are only a few examples of the hard work done by our predecessors and those leaders of our profession. So, how does your training program help the profession?
- The salesmanship of your efforts is a nice way to say that in our budget-guided world, proving that your training is sound, adequate, comprehensive, and realistic may mean the difference between gaining man-hours for training, promoting an officer to the training role, and acquiring a location to perform your practical training exercises.

Failure

We all have made mistakes, errors, and fumbles, and undoubtedly, we will make more of them. Failure is one of the overall reasons to train. Train so that your staff does not make mistakes. Train so that when mistakes are made, the correct quick reaction fixes the problem. Train so that when mistakes are made, the staff person who made the mistake can be given remedial training so that the mistake is not made again.

Failures are not always just failures. We can learn what works and what does not. We can put processes in place to counter the possibility of failure. And we can grow from failure through training.

Your department probably does not consider failure acceptable. This simple fact should amplify the need for providing minimal training to minimize the chance that failure will follow.

- Failure to recognize opportunities has troubled businesses for centuries.
- Failure to quit a poorly executed initiative has cost more than just dollars.
- Failure of will to see a complicated effort to the end.

- Failure of trust in your staff and the training you provided will cause undue effort and consternation.

Failure, though not a pleasant topic, is a key reason to have available a sound and comprehensive training syllabus for your staff and organization. We do not want to fail. We do not want to deal with failure. We do not want to explain the cause of the failure. So, train in that failure is mitigated through hours in a classroom, tactical exercises, or roundtable discussions. Recognizing the potential for failure is the backbone of organizational resiliency. Our profession requires that we observe operations with an eye toward what can break, what portion is weakest, what requires additional safety measures, and what requires additional assets to remove a potential failure.

You should know by now that we are in the business of failures. We look for them, we document them, we measure failures, and we provide solutions to bolster the organization's resiliency to failure. All resiliency processes have a substantial failure identification and training component to compensate for failures.

From a leadership role, learning to deal with failure and regain organizational trust is another learning opportunity. Not all of us deal with failure well. But we can be trained to handle it professionally and clinically so that our actions bolster the organization as it deals with the failure.

Failure is the opportunity to begin again more intelligently.

Henry Ford

SUMMARY

You should have enough information from the above section to start selling your idea for a training program. You should put the reasons to train together with your organization's specific needs. Allow your audience to develop the want to see success and to assist in this endeavor. The more robust the organization's training acumen becomes, the less effort should be needed to seek future monies and budgets.

2

What Budget Items Do You Need to Consider?

INTRODUCTION

You now have a good sales pitch, but before asking for money, people, and equipment, having and being able to present a polished and well-formulated request has professional value. Think of when someone tries to sell you something without being shown what you are buying. If you are a savvy buyer, you know what you are buying. But if the person authorizes your training budget from your request, it is best not to take a chance that they do not understand what you are asking.

What You Need to Include in Your Training Budget

Your budget request will follow the training you are recommending for the staff. If that training is small or short-lived, then the budget will follow. However, if the training is a security academy, firearms training, self-defense, or another lengthy coursework with the requirements of equipment, specialized space, and specialized trainers, then the budget will be hefty and in need of strong documentation.

Before working on the budget, let us identify what you will require for your training event. As stated earlier, you need a well-written scope of work for the training event. If you have jumped into writing your curriculum and developing coursework, you are on the right path.

DOI: 10.4324/9781003292586-4

People

In the budget, there should be several line items that account for personnel to provide, develop, research, review, present, and take the training.

- Someone on your staff who understands your training needs and has the capabilities of documenting and delivering your training. Depending on the course you are planning, this could be an existing person who can do the work and spare the time from other activities or hire another with the skills necessary to do the work. Within the budget, if you are considering taking a person from one position to a new position, what will be required to replace the tasks they were performing, even if on a part-time basis?
- The scope of the training event, size of your operation, and geographic locations factor into determining if it is necessary to hire additional staff to ensure that the legal issues of each municipality are covered in the training.
- Trainers and curriculum development personnel can be the same people; however, if the training is to be delivered through provided courseware, the actual training may be completed by an existing supervisor with the applicable skills, thereby saving a little of the budget request and giving the existing employee somewhat of a promotion or title change.
- Should the training be specific to licensing, the need to pay a certified instructor may be required.
- If the course material needs to be re-trained on a cyclic basis, planning for additional personnel or manhours from an existing supervisor to provide the training should be considered.
- If your organization has an existing training or employee development department, your needs may be able to be assumed by that department with the need for oversight and course review still falling to your staff.
- If you find that you will need to hire for the position, develop a job description and contact your human resources to determine an acceptable wage and benefits for the perfect candidate.
- Estimate the time it will take to develop the curriculum and associated courseware.

Labor Hours

Have a rough figure as to what your organization needs to meet the training objectives and how many people it will take to develop the course material and then deliver and receive the training. Yep, each of your staff that needs to take the training will need to have labor hours budgeted to fulfill the training.

- When your staff attends the training event, it is labor hours away from their normal duties. Accounting for how many labor hours per staff member who will be attending the training is critical to a complete budget.
- Accounting for labor hours attributed specifically to training is a perfect example of auditing evidence to prove training was performed.
- Again, if your organization has an existing training or employee development department, they may be able to assist with their current methods of accounting for staff time while attending training.
- Doing the math for a single training event will add up quickly, having the plan to minimize the labor hours without minimizing the training needs may be one of your greatest hurdles and assets.
- Training takes time and in the case of firearms and other critical task training, making acceptations is dangerous both physically

Number of staff members required to carry a firearm:	A	
Basic firearms safety class:	8 hours x A = B	
Basic Marksmanship (Range time) class:	8 hours x A = C	
Initial training per officer	B + C = D	
Labor hours budgeted for class	A x D = E	
Replacement of overtime labor hours for staff while staff is undergoing the training	E x 1.5 = F	

Every marksmanship class will require certified Instructors for Basic Firearms Safety Classes:

Number of Range Safety Officers required per Basic Marksmanship Class (1 for every 4 shooters)

Range safety officers	A / 4 = G	
Instructor labor hours		16
Range set up hours		2
Range safety officer labor hours	G x 8 = H	
Total Training staff hours	E + F + H +16 +2	

Figure 2.1 An example might be firearms training.

and legally. In this case, do the labor-hours math and have your argument ready for needing the training and not minimizing the training because of cost (Figure 2.1).

Equipment

Equipment and materials to conduct a training event are essential to ensure understanding and retention. Learning is accepted at a better level when conducted in an appropriate venue which could mean tail-gate training at a construction site, or comfortable chairs with available drinks in a lengthy classroom session. The following are a few ideas when asking for equipment costs.

- Should your training event be conducted in lecture only, there is a good chance that requesting equipment costs may be at a minimum as most organizations have other training events and the materials are already allocated. Equipment such as projector, screen, laptop, whiteboard, flip paper pads, easel, markers, and notepads – these are the economic norm. More advanced memory whiteboards, though more expensive, can bring a technology flair if used appropriately.
- If training will be conducted in the field, a small monitor or laptop may work; however, testing this is important because if the staff member cannot hear or see the presentation due to environmental issues, the training event is a bust. The full concentration of the student is critical to ensuring comprehension and some sort of short quiz is to ensure retention.
- Most organizations conduct training and share conference rooms replete with projectors and screens. Scheduling uninterrupted time for using the room and equipment should be an easy task.
- Handouts are generally easily printed and published in-house. If the handout will be used throughout the staff members' employment, professionally published handouts will be easier to maintain. However, recognize that the information imparted during the training may require special handling and protection. Keeping handouts generic in terminology is a good way to allow for the open distribution of materials.
- Not all training can be conducted solely by lecture. The need for the staff members to understand the content may require discussion, team building, self-study, or group projects. These

forms of training will require materials of a different style than normal handouts. This form of training may also require the instructor and any assistants to practice the course to ensure a manageable student body and that the results are those sought by the course objectives.

- Training events that require specialty equipment have a higher price tag and budgeting needs further thought. Self-defense equipment, handcuffs, weapons training, and firefighting skills testing all require additional technical equipment as well as support personnel.
- Should a need arise that actual on-duty equipment be necessary to conduct the training, such as various personal protection equipment (PPE) or other equipment typically in short supply such as weapons, consider the entirety of your operation when choosing to take materials from your on-duty staff to conduct the training. Using these pieces of equipment means that the on-duty staff may not have them available should a need arise while the training is being conducted.
- Firearms training requires a secure lecture space and firing range. Costs regarding the range should be budgeted to include ammunition, possibly firearms rental, safety gear, and targets. Look for a range that bundles such costs together per shooter.
- For training events such as firearms and self-defense, having a shared capability with another agency or organization can minimize costs. However, relationships sometimes sour, or space not in your control can be reallocated leaving your training budget to suffer. Also remember that if you borrow another agency's space, you may need to reciprocate.
- Budgeting for self-defense training will probably require padded targets, heavy bags, replica weapons (blue guns), and space for safe defense practice.
- If your organization has a training department, get them involved and see if some of your budget needs can be absorbed by that department. Your training needs may make their department larger which could be a feather in their cap. However, be cautious that your department's training needs do not take a backseat to the needs of other departments.
- Should the training event require a certified instructor, such as National Rifle Association (NRA) certified instructors or American Heart Association (AHA) CPR instructors, to list a

few, ensure those costs are included in the budget. You may also find that a member of your organization holds the needed certification as an instructor.

- Depending on the size of your budget, allocating time and money to get a member of your staff certified to provide training, such as Taser™, or CPR and first aid will reduce costs in the long run and include personal accomplishment for the staff member.

Certification Costs

An option for increasing the professionalism of your organization and the furtherance of security as a profession, you may consider providing coursework so that your staff members can test for certification.

- Obtaining certification is not a given. It includes considerable time to study and may require coursework followed by success-fully taking an examination to prove understanding and reten-tion of the material. A common problem is that security professionals know the information through experience, but the need to put that experience into wording and terminology used by the certification body is troublesome. Taking the time to ease your staff member's fear of testing is critical to hurdling this common problem.
- Some certifications have a two or three-year expiration with the need to collect additional training to retain the certification. In future budgets, you will need to account for this time and cost.
- One comment on certifications is that once received they belong to the person who took the test. There is a benefit to your staff holding several certifications, but if they move on to a position that assists with their career goals, the certification goes with them. Therefore, explaining to the staff member that it is in their best interest to pay for and gain the extra training, with your company paying for select events when it is in the best interest of the organization.

HOW TO SET UP A BUDGET

You have a list of hours required of your staff to attend the training, the number of employees you will need to hire and an estimate of what that will cost, a list of required equipment and their associated costs, and the time to develop the courseware and preparation for the training. Now it is time to develop your budget document.

- Check to see if your accounting department has tools to assist with your efforts, and familiarize yourself with the budget planning calendar so you will know at what date you will need to sell the idea so that you can move forward with budgeting. If the budgets are required by October 30, then you need to start developing your budget at least by the beginning of October. And the selling of your idea should start well before that. Surprise large budget line items rarely get funding.
- Check to see if your accounting department has a budget checklist or planning document. Do not waste time setting up a budgeting template if accounting has one that is required to be used.
- If this is your first time developing a new budget, the most common method is known as bottom-up estimating.
- The bottom-up process starts with a statement of work, which you should have from your course objective that started this effort.
- Develop a calendar of events with milestones. Since the budget will be spread across the time from development to the actual training, the spending will be parsed out from accounting based on these milestones.
- Take the costs you have put together and insert them into the appropriate milestone. When budgetary dollars are granted, the accounting department will not only need to know how much will be required over the year but at each milestone. This allows them to only make available the money needed for a month at a time.
- Since security is typically a cost-center, chances are you will not be able to show a profit but you can enumerate the benefits of a well-trained staff when it comes to customer service and fewer staff errors.
- If you already have a training program and you are just advancing what you already have established, demonstrating the delta can be seen as a profit or positive outcome of the spending.
- New budget items sometimes require that a five-year projected budget accompany the budget for this year so that management can see a more total cost of the event. Since training is necessary and constant training is your goal, project the costs as a separate line item.

- January – Search for and Hire Training Coordinator $_____
- February – Initiate Curriculum Development $_____
- March – Peer review and management review of curriculum $_____
- April – Edit course and develop courseware – Identity and Order equipment $_____
- May – Receive equipment and publish courseware $_____
- June – Schedule and start training $_____
- July – Training $_____

Figure 2.2 Milestone budgeting.

- In future budgets, remember that salaries and expenses tend to increase, so ensure if forecasting for multiple years in the original request document, costs reflect any increases.
- Equipment used in training is meant to take the abuse of training so that real equipment is not damaged. Therefore, count on replacing some items annually, such as striking pads and protective equipment (Figure 2.2).

SUMMARY

Drafting a budget for your training project, regardless of size, is an executive effort. Your documentation will demonstrate maturity and a deep understanding of the processes to perform a new task with the basics of organizational resources.

Your budget document should cover the need for equipment, personnel resources to develop and train, as well as the allocation of staff time to attend the training. Confer with your accounting department about the organization's common negotiation practices such as asking for more than is needed with the intent to accept and get by with less, or starting small with the intent to increase the budget in future years. Both of these tactics are common, but more important is to determine when the training you need to provide must be developed and presented. If this training effort is due to a recent state law change, then immediacy should be identified and the budget negotiations minimized.

3

Development of Training Coursework

INTRODUCTION

Reading this text proves that you believe in training your staff as an important function of your position, the organization, your staff's safe performance, and the profession. In any endeavor, moving forward with an idea but without a plan is foolhardy and fraught with failure.

"We need a plan!"

ADDIE

Welcome to the world of curriculum development and instructional system design. Yes, what you are striving to do is a system approach to training. Like most systems, it will start with a plan that includes analysis, design, development, implementation, and evaluation. A faithful and long-lasting cycle from the US military known as ADDIE (Analyze, Design, Develop, Implement, and Evaluate).

Analysis of the training needs of your organization. Starting with the state of your current training.

- Are you already providing training but lack the background documentation?

DOI: 10.4324/9781003292586-5

- Have you purchased a prepackaged training course that you find inadequate for your organization but used as a basis for your training?
- If you have training, is it adequate or just good enough and then must spend hours with new employees to explain why they do the things your organization requires?
- Are too many errors being made by your staff that can be remedied by a better training opportunity?
- What training and training standards are required by your industry and legal requirements?

Design the training curriculum to fit the needs of the organization, and its staff capabilities. Included in the design should be thought and planning to include a schedule that enables the security department to train with minimal impact on deployment through scheduling and costs.

Develop the course materials in a concise method so that additional instructors can be developed, and that each instructor teaches the same materials. And develop all testing events so that they are constructed to be educational, and a measure of the information's usability and retention.

Implement the training events so the curriculum is compounding and the best use of lecture, self-study, application, practice, and testing.

Evaluate the student's success, the instructor's capabilities, the material's worthiness, the long-term retention of the materials, and the usefulness in varied events where the instructional basis is utilized to solve problems. Evaluate the critical thinking component so that the basic course allows for the student to utilize what was learned during complicated or stressful events.

The curriculum development process is ongoing, or as you might find ever-growing and consuming. From the beginning steps in analyzing and identifying what topics to train and the continuous manipulation of that information while developing and molding it into a formattable course. Then the preliminary delivery of the course to adjusting the tempo, content, and attributes to ensure comprehension. Followed by implementing the training course with scheduling and classroom management and continuing with multiple levels of evaluation to ensure course effectiveness. Then, start the cycle again, though on a limited basis, as the process continues until the course is deemed unneeded and shelved.

Similar to the policies, procedures, and processes of your organization, the curriculum is a living, breathing, and ever-changing entity. It requires heavy documentation, and from the start, it will require constant research, reviewing, updating, additions, and reworking.

The weight of training documentation has several purposes: evidence of training, proof of due diligence, and salesmanship of your efforts.

- Evidence of training can be subpoenaed to verify that the staff member received the required training and that the training received was the same as those in other classes. Therefore, ensure that each of your officers receives the same training and that each officer can perform in the same position with similar quality of that performance.
- Evidence of equity and unbiased staff development.
- Evidence to protect your staff member's actions and mitigate potential legal issues to justify their actions.
- Due diligence that your organization provides training similar to that of your peers and meets the legal requirements of your organization's industry and municipal codes.
- Justify the validity and necessity of the training you provide by offering proof with statistics of fewer errors, commendations for professional service, and both internal and external comments.

Security needs to be consistent across the organization. Therefore, consistent and well-documented training removes ambiguity within your processes. The goal would be that each officer performs the same task to the same level to ensure your security protocols are being followed.

In all organizations, employees, customers, and visitors may look to side-step security for their individual benefit. Therefore, that person will look for the shift, post, or officer that will look past small insecure activities such as not wearing a badge, holding an access-controlled door for another entrant, or stepping out for a cigarette while blocking a door open.

Training events help ensure that all staff receive the same training and that they comprehend the training material and its importance. It is vital to remove the potential for security breaches by a staff member who might look the other way and allow this type of infraction.

Should your organization require that your staff be placed in positions that require specific training, such as carrying a firearm, lifesaving efforts, fire system inspections, patrol procedures, Global Security Operation Center (GSOC) operations, or emergency responses, the criticality here is ensuring no staff member fills a billet before having the requisite training in these vital and critical security operations. Most recently in the news, training proof can be subpoenaed or become part of an inter-organization review should a security event and the subsequent actions and response of your staff be questioned or deemed to end in a poor result. Proving that the methods used by your staff were correctly administered can save your organization's reputationally, financially, and legally.

Of course, maintaining training records and curriculum development research is often required under many regulations governing security activities and any certifications to which your organization conforms, such as the Hospitalization Insurance Portability Act and Accountability (HIPAA), Statement of Standards for Attestation Engagements 21 (SSAE21), or International Standards Organization (ISO) certifications for information networks, or quality assurance. If your organization reports that training is completed and that the training is the current norm for other organizations, then proof will be necessary to pass audits and thereby maintain certification.

In the security profession, understanding, and accepting methods to mitigate risk are one of the legs on which we stand. Protection if incorrectly performed can cause the greatest risk to the organization. Therefore, ensuring your department is afforded the best training from the candidate's initial company orientation to the daily tasks and even the crisis-level efforts should be your goal.

If a specific risk is identified and your efforts to mitigate that risk are not a topic of your staff's training, there is a weakening in the efforts to reduce the risk. In legal parlance, your efforts to counter the risk are lacking and may not be in keeping with the efforts and practices of others in the same business or industry of your organization. By not acting with due diligence to counter the threat, you are placing your organization at risk of that threat and the risk of litigation, reputational harm, or worse. An egregious example would be arming your officers without providing adequate weapons handling, characteristics, functioning, and marksmanship training, and your organization's policies regarding the proper use of force, and testing their proficiency in these subjects.

Assume that you already understand the need for training your staff, what subjects need to be taught, which subjects require just an understanding, which require proof of competence, and which require practiced movements. However, for the documentation required in curriculum development, you will need to research the reasons for the topics and the level of competence. Some of these reasons will be easy:

jurisdictional requirements by law, findings received after completing a risk assessment or security survey, or while researching and interviews done in the completion of the task analysis. Determining competence levels may be a little harder but research will guide your efforts. An example of competence level determination might be, if your staff members carry firearms then the competency in marksmanship might equal that of the local police department's quarterly firearm with a minimum qualifying score of 85%. Allowing your organization to qualify with less frequency or less accuracy could lead to legal issues. And if the municipal law governing armed security requires qualifying quarterly, or maybe annually, with a qualifying score of 75%, your organization may want to require the same. Or an optimum allowance that your organization strives for a higher training score that matches that of the local law enforcement.

TRAINING TOPICS

Introduction

In our profession, a basic security academy, new hire orientation, cyber security for non-cyber folks, report writing, evidence handling, introduction to risk, conducting security audits, intelligence modeling, and customer service tactics are just a few of the courses and training topics you might want to formulate and develop training curriculums for your organization.

New Hire Orientation

If you are drafting training for a new hire orientation then your topics might include emergency egress, how and when they can access the facility, how guests are treated, treatment and handling of badges and keys, their role in security, and more. The orientation might include a walk-through of the facility explaining entrance and exits, what to do and what is considered unacceptable behavior, where to park, how to bring in products, and whom to call for assistance.

The new hire orientation is a perfect opportunity to make a good impression and ensure that the new hire does not see you as a threat but as a co-worker with the same set of goals allowing them to work in a safe and secure environment.

Based on the security level of your organization or specific facilities that your organization operates, new hire orientation might have different flavors. A security opinion is that most new hire orientations are not sufficient to train candidates. The test for this occurs when a recent hire exits an emergency exit-only door or walks into a critical area where they were forbidden because the door was ajar, who is at fault? One training formula is if the security of your operation is important then the same importance should be placed on the amount of time and effort put into the new hire training.

Example:

- Start the new hire orientation by gathering the information security needs for recall of employee information, emergency contact information, email address, phone number, department, immediate supervisor, vehicles driven, and the like.
- Have the new hire read and sign a security statement covering the important highlights and have the candidate sign that they understand and will comply with the security requirements.
- Produce and present a short video or graphic presentation covering all the important highlights that the new employee just covered. However, this presentation allows for a lengthy question-and-answer period to ensure the new hire is comfortable and understands the security policies and practices.
- Conduct a walk-through with the new hires covering the use of badge, biometrics, and approval process for access to special areas, bathrooms, conference rooms, break rooms, parking, gates, and their specific work area with a final handoff to their immediate supervisor. The customer service value to security taking time spent making sure they are comfortable with the security practices of the company has great value. (See Section II, Chapter 6 for New Hire Orientations.)

Security Academy

Topics taught during an academy can be as robust as your organization requires. Wearing the uniform, manner, and bearing expected of security, shift requirements, break periods, the chain of command, introduction to legal terms, criminal law, civil law, patrol procedures, post orders, use of force, responding to an active shooter, radio codes, and more. (See Section II, Chapter 6 for more on security academy topics and task analysis.)

Policies, Procedures, and Processes

Often overlooked but as security is responsible for ensuring that policies are followed, it is most important that your staff have a complete knowledge and understanding of the policies they enforce.

On-the-Job Training

Often, what is taught in an academy is not what your staff will perform daily. Providing specifics as to what the staff member is expected to do and to what level of performance is critical to ensuring they start with a firm grasp of their job. (See Section II, Chapter 7 for more on security field training and on-the-job training.)

Curriculum Development Terminology

Using the correct terminology for Instructional Systems Development (ISD), curriculum development, and technical training will assist in understanding any article or conversation with others doing similar work.

Lesson Guide

The Lesson Guide, also known as a Lesson Topic Guide, is the instructors' portion of your training curriculum. It gives a listing of objectives that the course or a portion of the course will cover and an outline to ensure that each instructor teaches and trains the same information in each course given. It will look like an outline with short statements covering the content and it is then up to the instructor to expound upon the information. If you are fortunate to have several instructors, each should have a personal copy so that it can be annotated with anecdotes. Stories and examples that help the instructor assist the students in remembering or understanding a topic. In practical training, the Lesson Guide would give performance and practice steps, mirrored in competency testing.

Student Guide

This can be a very valuable piece of your courseware. The student guide assists the student with the meter and direction of the lesson while using simple questioning techniques so that the student can listen, understand, and be able to complete the pages as the lesson progresses. There are some considerations as to the academic level of your staff. Should the guide be drafted too elementary or too advanced your staff may not be able to follow along. Therefore, ensure the guide is developed at a level commensurate with the average student taking the course.

NOTE:
The information in the student guide may be considered "company private" as the information is how your security department operates. Protection of the student guide may be required by markings and warnings to the students (Figure 3.1).

Objectives

There are three types of objectives: Course Objectives, Terminal Objectives, and Learning Objectives. In the strictest of training environments such as formal military training, these objectives are fully flushed statements that can be almost a full paragraph and list the behavioral outcome of the learning. Your writings may not need to be as formal a statement of the objective as the importance lies with identifying the purpose of each section of the training, how it will be taught, and what will be required of the student to prove that they know the material.

The objectives will be listed at the beginning of the lesson so that the students understand what will be covered and thereby prepare them for the training. Objectives are placed for flow, cadence, and complexity. A simple outline form would look like this:

Course Objective
    Terminal Objective
        Learning Objective
        Learning Objective
        Learning Objective
    Terminal Objective
        Learning Objective

Example:
Introduce the legal aspects of the Security Officer's position, including authority, sources of law, common law, criminal law, and civil law.

Provide an understanding of how information is critical to the day-to-day efforts of the organization. Information has certain values, and the organization has methods of sharing information. Discussions during this session include how Security communicates within the department, and how Security personnel should handle the acceptance and delivery of protected information.

Define the difference between Crime and Loss Prevention, and how Loss Prevention is the furtherance of security to protect the interests of the organization and its clients for which they work.

Lesson Objective

The purpose of this class is to acquaint and provide the Security Officer with an understanding of the legal aspects of their position. This session will cover authority, sources of law, common law, criminal law, and civil law.

Enabling Objectives

1.   *Authority as a Security Officer*

2.   *Sources of Law*

3.   *Crime Defined*

4.   *Types of Law*

5.   *Nevada Criminal Law*

6.   *Civil Law and Security*

1.   *Authority as a Security Officer*

  a. *State of* _____

  State laws require that the following types of Security Officers must comply with specific laws about the position:

  _____

  _____

Figure 3.1   Student guide example.

Before work begins, officers in the above types of Security Positions must

complete:

_____

_____

b. *Proprietary Security Officers, also known as* _____

   Security Officers who are not armed and have no specific regulations or

   laws to follow.

   (Organization) Security Officers are _____ *Officers.*

c. *In some cases, Security Officers may have Police Officers' Powers to Arrest.*

   Security Officers at (Organization) have _____ *Powers*

   to Arrest.

d. *Differences between Police and Citizen Powers to Arrest*

   • *As a Security Officer at (Organization), you **cannot** legally make*

      an arrest for _____ *Cause.*

   • *You **cannot** arrest a person for a* _____, *even if you have*

      knowledge that one exists.

   • *And as a Security Officer you have no* _____ *to Arrest.*

2. *Sources of Law*

   a. *There are four sources of Law.*

   b. _____ *Law   (Based on English Law) "thou shalt not"*

   Examples: Murder   Theft   Rape

   State _____ _____ *have Common Law.*

Figure 3.1   (*continued*)

c. _____ Law

    Also known as Written Law

Statutes are defined as laws which are passed by the Federal

_____ *and State* _____. *These statutes are the basis*

for Statutory Law.

The Legislatures pass statutes that are later put into the Federal code of

laws or pertinent State code of laws.

Statutory law also includes local _____, *which is a statute*

passed by a county government to guard areas not covered by Federal or

State. Commonly, these are called _____ *codes.*

d. _____ Law

Judge makes an _____ *of law, and that decision becomes*

the acceptable definition until another judge makes a change.

In Latin, this is known as _____ _____ *which means*

"Let the decision stand".

e. _____ Law

This is the fundamentals of US Law

Bill of Rights: Was written to protect the _____ *from the government.*

The rights outlined in the Bill of Rights are _____ *and cannot*

be revoked.

Figure 3.1 (*continued*)

Introduce the Security Officer to the importance of gathering evidence and how evidence should be handled. And, on a larger scale define incident scene preservation and when and in what circumstances dictate when an incident scene should be preserved.

Course Objective

A course objective is a statement identifying what you want your personnel to learn during the entire course. As this covers an entire course or a section of a total course, it can be lengthy. To start, write a list of everything covered in the course and put that into sentence and paragraph format.

The course objective should also give a reason or cause for the course and motivators as to why your personnel would want to pay attention to the course. You probably already know that adults learn differently than children. Adults want to know why, and this is a positive attribute as to how the material will be used and the benefit of learning the material gives purpose and increases retention of the material.

Terminal Objective

The terminal objective is the culmination of a set of learning objectives for one lesson. A lesson covering an introduction to civil and criminal law might have a learning objective of criminal law definitions, one on civil law definition, and one on similarities and differences between both.

Example:

The student will be introduced to basic criminal code terminology including the definitions of common crimes, the different forms of intent, the difference between a crime and a tort, definitions of common civil torts, and the applicability of these definitions to the security department.

A learning objective, or enabling objective, is a statement as to what needs to be taught and to what level of comprehension in a specific section of the terminal objective. In the example above, there may be a learning objective for common crimes, common torts, forms of intent, and applicability to security.

Example:

The student will be able to identify a list of common crimes with their definitions by pairing them in a list with 100% accuracy.

Task Analysis

The task analysis is a formal document that identifies what is to be taught, the reason for the training, and most importantly, the justification for the training. As mentioned above, municipal codes can be a good justification and so can human resources directives, legal counsel recommendations, company practices, and standards with which the company complies. There are many more, but the task analysis is the basis for every training lesson.

Why would you need your staff to be able to define criminal and civil issues:

- Use the correct terminology,
- Increased knowledge of the criminal justice process, and
- A basis for their position.

4

Legal Training Requirements, Gap, and Task Analysis

INTRODUCTION

Security personnel perform a variety of roles. Yes, there are still organizations that hire contract security companies to provide personnel to either augment their security staff or perform the entire security function for the company. There are also proprietary or in-house security teams that provide a varied function within the organization. Both forms of contract and proprietary security personnel have specific legal requirements required by a state agency and some also must adhere to municipal codes.

In-House Security and Contract Security

Most state-mandated security training requirements are drafted to protect the end user of the security service. Since the end user is hiring a company to provide security staffing there needs to be a trust that the contracted security staff have a basis of security knowledge and a clean criminal background. The training requirements are somewhat basic as compared to those an organization requires of its personnel, but training requirements seem to be growing in recent years. It should also fall to the

DOI: 10.4324/9781003292586-6

company hiring the contract security force to require special training if necessary for the positions the contract personnel will fill.

In-house should at a minimum follow their state and municipal requirements for training of contract officers, but this is only the beginning.

Using common security terms, there are two basic types of security forces:

Contract Security is where a company provides security personnel as a security force to an organization.

Proprietary or In-House Security is where the organization hires direct employees as a security force for their organization.

These two types of security forces generally have a difference in regulatory mandates. For example, in general, a contract security officer must take a state-required course, successfully pass a test, be fingerprinted, and have a background investigation to ensure no criminal history exists. The intent of this is to ensure that any organization that contracts with a guard company has some assurance that the officer providing security has basic knowledge and is without a criminal history.

In the proprietary instance, the officer is hired by the organization to which they protect. That organization conducts whatever training and background investigation it deems necessary for the officer's position.

Regardless of which or a combination of security forces your organization employs, this text will not attempt to document the differences between the municipal requirement for security as they are ever-changing and specifics of employment can require an in-depth knowledge of the statutes.

Armed and Unarmed

Most states have an armed officer training minimum as no legislator wants an untrained, armed officer in the public. Similar to law enforcement personnel taking and passing marksmanship courses to carry a firearm while on duty. Contract or in-house officers typically must comply with this same training.

Any security force personnel that carry a weapon needs to fully understand the purpose, capabilities, and use of weapons in the function of their position. As weapons can harm, hurt, or kill, some states put greater restrictive training requirements on those organizations and officers. In some cases, these training requirements do not regard a difference between contract and proprietary guard forces. These additional mandates should be researched and where necessary, reviewed with legal counsel to ensure the training of your staff is appropriate and in compliance.

Contractual Requirements

There is a great possibility that you may be entering this training development endeavor in multiple stages of the process. You may already have a new hire orientation, some level of security academy, and a handful of specific practice or process training programs. You may have contracted CPR/first aid/automatic electronic defibrillator (AED), and/or weapons training. Regardless of where you are in the whole process of setting up a training program for your department, it is recommended that you first take a step back and do a review of your needs. This foundational research will assist in budgeting and giving a firm vision for your staff's training.

The varied roles and legal identities are proof that the next step in your curriculum development will be your own as none will be the same. The entry-level definitions and actions may be similar but the roles your personnel perform are different than others. This can be through the combination of roles or specializations required of your department.

GAP ANALYSIS

A gap analysis is a process where you list the current training and the list of needed training to provide a focused picture of what curriculum needs to be developed. Starting with a few lists.

- List what training is already documented and is currently being provided to your staff. Adding any side notes such as shortfalls in the training that you see, or problems that others may have identified with the current curriculum.
- List what training you would like to see and that you have deemed necessary for your department personnel to receive. Add notations such as how you see this being performed. Add to this list the basis of regulatory needs, what training your peers provide their staff, and the highest goals you have for your department personnel to achieve.

These two lists will make up something called a gap analysis. Where your training program currently sits, and where you envision it needs to be is the gap. The breadth and depth of that gap are completely in your hands but you need to be brutally honest with your assessment, regardless of the effort to minimize the gap.

Now within the gap analysis document, list to the side, all stake-holders for each training item. These stakeholders can be customers (contractual requirement imposed on your department), other inner organizational departments (area of classified material handling due to the materials that may require additional first aid training for exposure, extra patrols, or technology to limit access), or specific groups within your department (the intelligence unit within your department required additional access control).

Two more critical items need to be added to your gap analysis document: List any constraints to fulfilling your dream security training curriculum.

- Time-related items are common and might include an estimated time to develop the courseware, current budget shortfalls, and time until the next budget review period.
- Assets and locations that are required to provide the training, such as a firearms range, classroom, computer needs, legal review, and publications.

Lastly, the gap analysis should identify the current academic level of those to be trained. This portion of the analysis may have several levels. A new hire orientation should be provided at the lowest level to allow for any person, possibly including non-security personnel, to successfully comprehend and perform to the needs of the organization. And, course-work such as intelligence gathering and modeling may require higher written communication skills. Other requisite skills may include oral communication, a physical fitness level for specific tasks, or possibly licensing to drive specific levels of vehicles.

Depending on the size and composition of your department, it is recommended to get buy-in during this process. Ask your senior staff to perform their gap analysis or work as a team so the final product is a joint effort. This is especially important if your senior staff each have different roles in the operations, such as one handling classified materials, one having ownership of plant security, and another specific to executive protection.

Putting all this information into document form should be a hallmark of your department's new training development goals. Provide a copy to upper management and your department's key personnel so they know of your vision to train staff to be the best they can be and perform in a manner prescribed by your organization's principles and strategy.

One important note of the gap analysis is that it is dated. Because as your vision becomes reality the gap analysis will change form.

- It will grow as you find critical training was missed on your first pass of the gap analysis.
- It will shrink as your training becomes real and staff becomes trained.
- It will evolve as your training efforts morph your department into a new organism where training is constant and consistent, staff members look forward to attending training, earning certifications, and becoming a greater part of your organization's security strategies.

SECURITY TRAINING NEEDS

Anyone in security knows that one cannot walk into this job without being trained as to their specific duties. And, you may already have a good grasp on what subjects should be included in the training you are developing; however, looking for empirical data on what training is necessary is a wise move.

There are several avenues that can be taken to determine what subjects your initial training should cover. You can choose to expound upon these in continuous training efforts.

- ASIS International's "Private Security Officer Selection and Training Guideline" dated 2004. And, the update "Private Security Officer Selection and Training Guideline" dated 2019.
- ASIS Foundation and University of Phoenix's "Enterprise Security Competency Model." This study which was endorsed by the US Department of Labor identified the key skills required to be a security officer and researched the direction of training to attain promotion.
- The workplace competencies, industry-wide technical competencies, and industry-sector functional areas are the most important to your list.

Professional Associations

- The International Foundation for Protection Officers (IFPO) specifically has certifications and training materials for the security officer, such as the Certified Protection Officer (CPO) certification.

- The ASIS International suite of certifications, specifically the recent Associate Protection Professional (APP).
- "The American Security Guard, Security Guard Training Manual," 2019 Edition from SecuriStart.
- "Practical Security Training" by Patrick Kane CPP, 2000.
- "The Protection Officer Training Manual," IFPO.
- Peer Review – borrow from your security peers, in your region and others in your type of industry. Your peers may have already done the research, and sharing assists in bolstering the strength of their program.

In our litigious world, when security is in question, a large value is placed on verifying the security practices, processes, and training that your organization subscribes to was verified through a process of due diligence, as to what is common in your industry. If all your peers lock the front doors after hours and your company does not, and an occurrence takes place based on your front door security practice, then you did not do your due diligence. The same goes for the training you provide. This is not to say that your peers are always correct in their manner; however, knowing and accounting for the difference in your practices may become important.

Having a thorough knowledge of security, its management, operational requirements, and the organization will give directions in identifying the training needs of your security department, but failing to conduct a formal task analysis may lead to a poorly developed curriculum. Developing a curriculum for an occupation is a business within itself and there are benefits to paying for such a service. More poignantly put, your knowledge of the complete security department's operations can be detrimental to the training due to the following:

- Without being snarky, you should recognize that your knowledge of security is coming from your current position in the organization, which may preclude you from knowing the specific tasks of your staff and the intricacies of their daily duties.
- Your knowledge comes from a single focal point, which can be a one-way street. There are multiple ways to explain and define security protocols, you must allow research to flush out the multiple aspects. If you find that your knowledge has enough depth, all the better.
- You may lack knowledge that is important to the varied aspects of your organization. Lose the hubris and look for the little things

that you did not know, do the research, talk to your peers, and review other training offerings.

- Your belief that a bit of knowledge should be easily understood or known to all without the need for explanation is wrong. Not everyone may understand the simplest notion of the objective of security. Therefore, explain and ensure each item that is considered by the analysis to be important, is taught with the same fervor and time as a more complicated function. An example might be crime definitions – when speaking to law enforcement, using incorrect terms and definitions can place your security staff in poor light with their law enforcement peers.
- Believing that a function or action required of your staff personnel should be considered common and not necessarily need to be trained will quickly leave you with more work. An example of this could be the marking of evidence. When an item of evidence ends up in trial, and the marking is inconsistent with your processes, or the lack of marking allows for the evidence to be dismissed due to a lack of chain of evidence. Do not take for granted that common tasks are known by trainees.

A common example of a daily occurrence: An officer is put at a post and is expected to perform well with little training specific to the position.

- Where are the issues that require the officer's attention?
- Does the gate have a problem closing too fast?
- What is the local chain of command?
- What executive or officials are expected to come through this post?
- Is that door always open?
- What if the delivery comes to this post – where are they directed?

We, humans, tend to overlook what is obvious to us and forget what a new person does not know or needs to be taught.

Example:
I was watching a contracted technician try to appease his supervisor in how to wrap an extension cord. He was told he did it wrong three times and had to figure out alternate methods of wrapping the cord. Afterward, I asked the supervisor how he was trained to wrap the cord, to which I was told: "he should know better." If such a skill is so important to the supervisor, would not a simple example have solved the problem and saved time and embarrassment?

ORGANIZATIONAL MANAGEMENT WANTS OF SECURITY

The easiest way to determine what your organization wants out of its security department is for one of your subordinates to make a mistake. Too late? Tongue in cheek, but it always seems to be the little events that put thoughts into what management wants out of security.

So, you need to ask the question of your most senior leaders, including legal and human resources. They may delegate the task to another but they cannot pass on the responsibility.

The question should not be simple; based on your experience with the organization, you should be able to come up with a list of tasks for which your officers are currently responsible. That list may surprise the organizational leadership. Putting together this list will help your question be usable and may answer an easier task (Figure 4.1).

Example:
What training can you determine is necessary for a staff member to be prepared to deal with the below events?

From my tenure in the profession, I have had many executives complain about an officer's tact, bearing, actions, complacencies, and basic attitude. Until I asked the question of executive, what do you want of security? You should know that they do not know what security does or how they do their job. That is why you were hired (feel the rush of power).

The following sections will be the heart of your organic research. Surveying your officers, conducting exercises with your supervisors, reviewing municipal requirements, asking your peers what training they provide, discussing the needs of company stakeholders, and examining any standards your company may follow.

List Every Duty Performed Based on the Interview

Let us assume that the organization's management wants your department to do its job. Absent a definition of that, may I suggest documenting what your officers do daily? Have your officers on all shifts and posts write down what they did as a rolling daily log? Receiving phone calls and answering intercoms can probably be captured as tick marks, but how many reports did they write, how many contacts did they make while on patrol, how many hours did they guard an open gate, how many cameras swept or door sensors did they check? Do they get the

SECURITY
COMMAND

	2021	2022
Access Granted	4	2164
Access Granted - Vendor	3365	3023
Camera Check	6310	6599
Customer Assistance	2192	4382
Customer Vendor Access	1847	3780
Equipment/Fire/HVAC Check	5	30
Escorts	1108	1099
Foot Patrols	9778	10444
Keys/Cards In/Out	1637	1421
Lost and found	21	26
Meeting/Tours	887	895
Orientation	307	417
Patrol Vehicle Fuel/Maintenance	99	70
Patrol Vehicle Inspection	303	812
Security Access Audit	214	286
Security Equipment In/Out	23	8
Security System Maintenance	6	19
Traffic Control	4	3
Vehicle Patrols	3064	2447

INCIDENTS

Access Violation	30	16
Alarm Violation	0	0
Assault	0	0
Auto Accident	4	1
Auto Break-in	0	0
Bomb Threat	0	0
Burglary	0	0
Civil Unrest	0	0
Earthquake	0	0
Employee Illness	0	1
Employee Termination	2	1
Equipment Problem - Facilities	44	37
Equipment Problem - Fire System	31	21
Equipment Problem - Network	6	2
Equipment Problem - Power	8	5
Equipment Problem - Security	41	19
Fight	0	0
Fire	2	0
Flood	0	0
Graffiti	0	0
Guest illness	1	0
Injury: Contractor	1	0
Injury: Customer	2	0
Injury: Employee	6	3
Injury: Guest	6	4
Injury: Vendor	1	0
Parking violation	4	1
Robbery	0	0
Suspicious	76	27
Theft	0	0
Trespassing	0	0
Trouble Call	1	2

Figure 4.1 Statistical data.

51

mail, pick up a food delivery, escort a guest, issue badges, attend training, or collect evidence?

While the officers are doing that, have your supervisors and managers do the same thing. Their list should include each time they needed to correct the response of an officer, give individual attention to an issue including the reason why, administrative tasks, inventories, overseeing, or checking posts.

Depending on the size of your department, an exercise can be done with supervisors regarding officers' responsibilities. Put the supervisors in a room and give them a pad of Post-its™. Give them a set time (maybe 15 minutes) to write every task their officers do, using one note per task. At the end of the exercise have the supervisors group their notes with notes from the other supervisors. Then correlate the notes on a single sheet to the tasks and a frequency to determine priority.

This exercise should give a realistic view of tasks performed and those tasks that require more supervision than others. If training can remedy some of the extra supervision, then there is a point toward additional training or a priority in the importance within the academy or on-the-job training.

Identify Incorrect Expectations

After asking what your leadership wants of the security department there may be a need to correct misconceptions about the roles of security. Specifically, leadership may believe security can do more than the law will allow, or breach the ethical standards of the profession.

It is common to hear others incorrectly discuss the role of your security department and its personnel. Whether the comments are derogatory "they are just for show" or egregiously incorrect "they shoot to kill." These types of comments are dangerous and potential litigation points when an event occurs with your staff. Correcting any mis-interpretation of the actions of your department is critical to the correct actions of your officers. Worse case scenarios may occur when a senior officer chasing a suspect, yells "Stop or I'll shoot" so the junior officer thinking that behavior is legal, fires a shot.

What could the result be if an executive boasts about potentially illegal actions and capabilities of the security staff, and it is overheard by a new officer, and that officer, believing the boast, tells others?

Incorrect expectations of a security department in technology or practice can be dangerous and lead to legal issues. Setting the records straight in your training of staff is an important factor in the training.

Discuss Findings with Legal and Human Resources

Discuss with human resources and legal department leadership after any additions and edits from your conversation with top management. Human resources and legal department leadership should answer your questions based on their roles, not misconceptions they may have formed.

Their answers should be documented and included as references, if possible. Know that there may be a difference of opinion between legal, human resources, and senior leadership. You will need to discern the right answer before moving forward with the training development. A legal interpretation, a definition from the workers' compensation insurance company, and a job classification description may alter the tasking of your department.

Hopefully, their responses will not be too far off, but every task adds to the training requirements, which if time allows is a positive to why you train your department. Examples can be report writing, testifying, soft skills, interviewing, and so on.

Both your organization's legal counsel and human resources departments are key stakeholders to your department and there is a good chance you already work together with them. Therefore, asking them what they feel are appropriate topics to train is a validation of the need for training and opens the door to advanced objectives.

Take the list of duties from the officer survey and supervisor exercise, combined with a lawful requirement imposed by the municipality and those topics that your experience has identified as necessary. Organize the notes and lists into a cogent set of course objectives for the stakeholders to review and approve. If comments arise from their review, note, and add the changes with their comments documenting the reasons for change.

Your training is also the perfect venue for the instruction of company policies and procedures. I think we all have had to sign that we have read and understand the company policy manuals without actually reading the manual. Security as the enforcer of policies needs to better understand these and be able to give guidance to other employees in their meaning.

FINALIZE THE TRAINING NEEDS

1. Complete a gap analysis of what is currently being trained and what additional topics need to be covered.
2. Develop a complete list of the current duties being performed by your security staff. If you oversee multiple security operations,

then look for synergies for the training curriculum and then list the additional duties separate by function.

3. Develop a list of what functions performed by security that your supervisory level staff members identify as necessary and of what importance.
4. Organize the tentative final list with the assistance and input of your senior staff.
5. Schedule and review the list with human resources, legal, and senior management for their input and approval. Maintain and documentation of approval or changes.
6. Re-organize the final list of topics for the training of your staff, into the Task Analysis.
7. Determine if the training should be comprehensive from the first day of employment or identify those topics to be trained once an existing staff member is promoted into other positions of security such as supervisor, trainer, executive protection, investigations, intelligence, and global security operations center operations.
8. Start at the beginning by developing course objectives for the new hires or other positions that have been deemed to need the most urgent training.

Remember to document the evolution of your list of topics and everyone's input. The documentation can be used to justify the need for budget, time, and personnel.

Consider some of the topics for continuous training for all your staff (discussed further in Section II, Chapter 8).

Get Signatures

When the final list of training topics is developed and in a training plan, review the list with each senior position from which you gained input and get them to sign the document. If asking for signatures is a problem, consider saving all correspondence (printed and electronic) regarding the activity.

5

Curriculum Development

INTRODUCTION

This section will deal with the actual training materials. This includes the course, lesson, and enabling objectives which can be either knowledge and/or skills objectives, a lesson topic guide (LTG), student guides, testing, and course evaluations. These are not the only components of a full course but they are the courseware that the students and instructors will handle.

In previous sections, we discussed objectives and their use as a selling tool to stakeholders to get the process started. Then conduct task analysis and research of what our peers and professional organizations are requiring, including your municipal governing bodies, and finally what your organization needs from its security staff. Merging the data, you should have come up with a list of knowledge and skills your staff will need to be introduced, trained, and practice a grouping of skills into a task analysis.

The skills then need to be put together in groupings of like knowledge and skills and those put into a flow of training starting with primary knowledge and skills, moving toward building and compounding skills and knowledge, and culminating in a completed objective. Not all topics will be compounding, such as first aid/CPR/automatic electronic defibrillator (AED) and others, as they can be stand-alone in nature and delivery. Though these may not fit in a progressive training course, the knowledge and skills can still be discussed as value that security provides the organization.

If your organizational security training needs are as complicated as most proprietary security, and contract security forces working within an organization as their security force, the list of knowledge and skills to be trained can be lengthy. Taking the list of topics and organizing them into a

DOI: 10.4324/9781003292586-7

flow from elementary knowledge to more complex information and then identifying a manner in which the topics can be taught while thinking of the operational tempo of your department. For example, is your organization large enough to absorb new hires directly into an academy format training curriculum upon hire and staying there until completed or is your operation such that your new hires need to be taught only what they need to be operational, with follow up on more advanced training once they meet other gates such and passing probation.

> NOTE:
> Ensure that no new hire is put into a position where they are subjected to a situation in which they have not been trained or not under direct supervision.

For this portion of the training planning, it is best to get input from your senior staff, as they are the ones responsible for the new hire while on shift and assigning supervision or on-the-job training personnel. During this part of the planning, consider identifying which senior manager would make a good trainer for certain topics as a passion for the topic may become evident.

Lastly, ask their opinion of which topic was better suited for on-the-job training or in the Field Training Program (discussed in Section II, Chapter 6 and 7). Some skills require repetition and an understanding based on more moving parts of the process than might be feasible in a classroom setting.

Having all the data, the entire course should be able to be put into an outline form and become the development schedule from the task analysis for the course being developed with associated courses to be developed at a later time to ensure inclusion in the complete curriculum.

DEVELOPING THE OBJECTIVES

Each of the main topic headings that your task analysis has identified now needs to be expressed as an objective. Before we get into developing learning objectives, we should come to an understanding of what an objective does. In this case, an objective is a goal or milestone in the training you have determined is necessary for your staff. In some high-level organizations and well-maintained training departments, the objective will tell the students what they are about to learn, what is expected of them, under what conditions, how they will be tested and what is a passing grade. I can tell you that if you write over one hundred objectives for your complicated courseware, they will soon all read the same. This does not remove the intent of the objectives, but it may give you a shortcut to the writing exercise.

In a formal training setting a learning objective may look like this example:

> *During this portion of the course, the student will learn the difference between crimes and torts (civil crimes) based on elements of the crimes and possible punishment and, given a list of definitions and a list of terms, the student will match the two listed items with 100% accuracy.*

If a single lesson has more than five learning objectives there is another method of listing the objectives. This method starts with a statement of purpose and then lists the main topics as subordinate objectives. The statement will list any conditions, testing, and measurements.

Example:

> *This lesson will discuss and identify the common crimes you might come across while working at the organization and have to investigate, document, and conduct investigations. After the below list of lessons, you will take a computer-based test regarding the below topics using various testing techniques requiring an 80% passing score.*

> - *Property Crimes, graffiti, destruction*
> - *Crimes of violence against a person*
> - *Crime of Trespassing*
> - *Property Crimes – theft*

> *The next set of lessons will discuss the relevance of the State criminal (penal) code, and how the specifics found in the code will help to identify the elements of the crime and how they can assist in your investigation to determine which subjection of the general crime has been committed and if the crime is a misdemeanor or felony. Using the current, issued State Criminal Code manual, identify the elements of specific crimes listed on the computer-based test with*

> - *Property Crimes, graffiti, destruction*
> - *Crimes of violence against a person*
> - *Crime of Trespassing*
> - *Property Crimes – theft*

Regardless of the method of documenting the objectives, this portion is important to formalize the task analysis into the plan for conducting the training. Listing the topics necessary for your staff is only one step in course development, now that listing needs to be put into a lesson with how the training will be presented, in what order, and what is expected of the student.

LESSON GUIDE

The document from which the instructor will teach and train your staff is the Lesson Guide, also known as an LTG. It will include the objectives, the task analysis, and a listing of subordinate materials and references that were used to build and develop a complete course, one lesson at a time (Figure 5.1).

The format of your LTGs should be standardized, but that can be any form that works for your organization. If your organization's training department already has a standard LTG format, your department should follow that. If not, above is an example, and below is a list of what should be included in the LTG.

- Course title
  This is the complete course, such as Security Academy or Leadership Training.
- Version number, original date, and date of any updates
  Your courseware will be in a constant state of flux as you or your staff find that processes have changed with your organization, the criminal code changes, or your team has taken on alternative tasks. Anytime there is a substantial change to the course, the version number should change with a new original date. However, if minor or editorial changes, such as phone numbers or room numbers are made, they can be done without changing the whole course document. They would be executed by making the changes to the course document, and any associated materials, and then date the change. It is recommended that a listing of these minor changes be made to the LTG, ensuring all copies of the LTG get changed. During the next rewrite of the course, those changes can be implemented.

  If your courseware, and specifically the LTG, is on a tablet or laptop, making changes is a little easier as making one change can edit all courseware. However, if your courseware is in paper

---

LESSON

1.1.1

==

PRIVATE SECURITY OFFICER AND THE CRIMINAL JUSTICE SYSTEM

Introduction:

References for this class: Company Security Policy (current date)

Company Security Access Control Procedures (current date)

Company Security Officer Position Description (current date)

State Criminal Code (current date)

"Blacks Law Dictionary" 11th Edition Thomas West, 2019

Lesson Objective

The purpose of this class is to acquaint and provide the Security Officer with an understanding of the legal aspects of their position. This session will cover authority, sources of law, common law, criminal law, and civil law.

Enabling Objectives

1.   *Authority as a Security Officer*

2.   *Sources of Law*

Figure 5.1   LTG example.

3.   *Crime Defined*

4.   *Types of Law*

5.   *Criminal Law*

6.   *Civil Law and Security*

Testing

A computer - based test will be given covering this portion of the course, using various

testing methods such as true/false, multiple choice, matching, and fill-in-the-blanks.
   90% accuracy is required.

Motivation

Get the students ready to learn with a motivational statement regarding the

importance of understanding the simplest portions of the law and how that pertains to the

company's security department.

1.   **Authority as a Security Officer**

a.   State laws where the company operates require that the following types of

Security Officers comply with specific laws about the position:

Contract   **Armed**

a.   Before work begins, officers in the above types of Security Positions must

complete:

Background Investigation   Work Card

Figure 5.1   (*continued*)

b. Proprietary Security Officers, also known as __In-House or Proprietary__ _____ Security Officers are not armed and have no specific regulations or laws to follow.

c. Our company Security Officers are __Proprietary__ Officers.

d. In some cases, Security Officers may have Police Officers Powers to Arrest.

e. Security Officers at the company have __Citizen__ Powers to Arrest.

f. Differences between Police and Citizen Powers to Arrest:

- As a Security Officer at the company, security **cannot** legally make an arrest for __Probable__ Cause.

- As a Security Officer at the company, security **cannot** arrest a person for a __Warrant__, even if you have knowledge that one exists.

- As a Security Officer at the company, you have no __Duty__ to Arrest.

2. **Sources of Law**

a. There are four sources of Law:

b. __Common__ Law (Based on English Law) "thou shalt not"

Examples: Murder Theft Rape

Figure 5.1 (*continued*)

form, following a change management system may be important. Since changes in the industry occur all the time, I recommend you print the current version for each class. Do not keep stacks of courseware which will be outdated by the latest changes.

- Lesson title/lesson number
  Title this lesson and give it a number based on previous and follow-on lessons. Using the X.X.X numbering works best.
    - X – Course
    - X.X – Lesson
    - X.X.X – Topic
- Reference materials
  List any reference materials that your staff can review to better understand a concept or specific information, such as Post Orders, Black's Law Dictionary, your State's Criminal Code, and your organization's policies, procedures, and other documentation.
- Course objective and subordinate learning objectives
  It is a great idea to explain to the students what they will learn in this course to prepare them for the lesson.
- Testing method and passing grade
  No surprise tests or test questions, communicating the topic items to the students so they will be aware of what they will be tested on and required to know to pass the course. You may need to explain other matters to assist the staff in understanding concepts, such as using stories and anecdotal comments. Anecdotes are not testable.
- Motivational statement as to why students need to learn this material
  Motivation can be found in the objectives, but the motivational statement by the instructor should be more of a personal statement as to why your staff should pay attention to the lesson, why they need to know the information, how it will be used in their daily tasks, how this portion of the course will be used in follow-on lessons, and other factors to motivate your staff to sit through the class, pay attention, retain the information, and be able to use it during their career with your organization.
- Lesson topic outline (LTG)/instructor comments
  The outline from the task analysis and any subordinate information the instructor feels will assist in explaining a concept to further understanding, increase comprehension and retention of the information.

The LTG documents how you have set the flow of the lesson, what items are introduced, and in what order.

An example of anecdotal information might be that during patrols, the officer is to check to ensure doors are locked. Depending on the type of locks installed at your facility you may need to describe the operation of certain locks, such as a classroom lock, privacy lock, deadbolt, maglock, and others.

The instructor comment section (not shown in the example) is for the instructors to list any example that assists with their ability to convey the information using analogies, or personal experiences.

If multiple instructors teach the lesson, a copy of the LTG can be made available for the instructor to annotate for their purpose with their examples. If all instructors use the same LTG, this section can include a list of examples that all instructors can utilize.

- Lesson review items (not shown in the example)
Without teaching the test, the instructor should know what material will be on the test, how it will be tested, and an example for the instructor to gauge comprehension before moving on to another lesson.

LTGs for skills lessons will take on a different look when it comes to any manipulative skill such as handcuffing, search, pat down, and patrol vehicle operations. The LTG outline is still necessary with all of the above components, but the description of the skills will be more complicated to document. Testing will also be different in that the tasks should be broken down so the instructor can grade a student's performance based on each step to be performed. In a handcuffing course, the steps to cuff from the standing position would include stance, control hold, cuff preparation, and drawing from the cuff holder.

STUDENT GUIDES/TAKEAWAYS

The experience level of your students will help to determine the type of student guide, handout, or takeaway for your course.

Student guides are typically developed using fill-in with statements, and sample test questions to ensure the student is following along with the class as well as minimizing notetaking to allow for the students' focus to be on the lecture. There are several drawbacks to student guides which will also demonstrate the need for variations and the use of multiple techniques in the development of the guide.

- Students and instructors can get too dependent on the guide. If the instructor gets carried away and continues with the lecture, the students may stop paying attention when they have lost their place in the guide. A student who is lost in what words should be inserted for fill-in-the-blank will stop the class to determine the inserted word, whether the student looks to another student for the word or asks the instructor. The momentum of the class is stunted, and the instructor must retrace their steps to fulfill the student's needs.
- Points to consider:
  - Are the students that you are training a type that is not well versed in taking notes and must follow along the best they can by only using the guide?
  - Was the course developed for one type of lecture and student capabilities, and was an alternate instructor unable to teach by the same methodology?
  - Should the student guide be rewritten to remove the distraction of filling in the blanks as the class is taught?
- Instructors can use different wording or vocabulary they are familiar with to teach the class, based on their education, experiences, or how they understand complex topics. Therefore, ensuring all instructors have a correctly complete student guide is essential so that all students receive the same education as well as being able to pass a test of the material.
- If the student guide is drafted with statements of knowledge that can be sample test questions, the development of those questions needs to conform to test question methodology. Whether in the student guide or test, statements or questions should not be drafted using double negative questions, no questions intended to deceive or reverse answers for true/false statements.
- The student guide should not be solely a pretest. Sample test questions on important topics can be added to ensure comprehension. A student guide filled with questions used directly on the test is known as teaching the test and is not advised in most academic forums.
- For those students who find notetaking as a learning tool, or as a kinesthetic learning activity, providing ample notetaking room is essential for ensuring that the course is developed for multiple types of student learners or academic levels.

- The material that your course covers can be considered company confidential, specifically when discussing processes used by your organization to protect people and property. Marking any take-away as such is important to maintain the protection of the process. However, seriously consider the actual need to place protected information in any student guide. If such a practice is required, consider collecting the student guides at the end of the course.
- When developing a student guide, consider varying the style of statements, note-taking, true/false, multiple choice, or read and underline. All of these will help the student remember, retain, and enable them to recall the material at a later time.
- Some short courses, such as new hire orientation or informational briefings may not need guides or testing; however, critical highlights can be bulleted on single pages and handed out near the end of the course.
- Consider a memento, souvenir, or tchotchke with an organizational and/or security logo as a takeaway to commemorate the employees' time. A new badge lanyard, coffee cup, stress ball, or other items can have a lasting effect on the student remembering the course.
- When conducting the initial teaching of a course it will be critical to ensure the student guide fits the needs of the learner. It may be too simple, at the wrong academic level, too complex, or the student guide is so important to the students' retention that it is more than a follow-along aide.
- Student guides for skills lessons are a part of the curriculum and will give the student the ability to remember key components of the skills to be learned. Such as various handcuffing techniques, your organization's use of force policy, or reminders of marksmanship techniques. Consider the student may not have a writing surface to complete statements or take sample test questions.

DEVELOP TESTING MATERIALS

I would bet that at one point in your life, you came across a test question that was intended to trick you. Whether the test question was written in the double negative, "Which one is not one of the correct answers" or a practical exercise where the tester removed a part or provided the wrong part during an installation to see if you noticed that the part was missing or incorrect. I can only guess that identifying the correct part was germane to the coursework or that at some point in the instructor's career, they faced a similar situation. However, if the objectives do not explain the reason for these types of questions, maybe the test developer was unskilled or untrained. Regardless, testing is a little science and a little art. And generally, trick questions serve no purpose.

For your reference library, there is a test development standard, the "Standards for Educational and Psychological Testing," a joint publication of the American Educational Research Association, the American Psychological Association, and the National Council on Measurement in Education (2014).

I imagine that there are subtopics in your curriculum that you might categorize as either good-to-know or nice-to-know. These subtopics assist in understanding complex ideas, such as case law regarding the crime of burglary, or anomalous indicators of a bad camera feed when troubleshooting a CCTV system. The good-to-know minutia may be important as it provides the student with a well-rounded understanding of the concept, but these are not the topics that your objectives have identified as being testable.

According to the test development standard above, there are several key points to developing test material:

- Define the purpose of the test,
- Develop and describe the knowledge and/or skills to be tested,
- Create a specification for testing,
- Draft potential test items and how the answers will be scored,
- Conduct and review pilot tests (yes, test the test), and
- Review and evaluate the quality of the test items and questions.

Define the Purpose of the Test

The most common form of testing is a written or computer-based test after a lecture or class. However, in the development of a security training department, there could be so much more than the simplest test. During on-the-job training your trainers will be testing the ability to perform the job, daily supervisors will assess the attitude of the trainee, aptitude for the tasks performed, full completion of the task, and general interest in the industry. More in-depth testing may include the ability to recognize hazards, use cognitive abilities to mitigate hazards, development of observation skills, as well as conflict resolution and specifics of the position that a trainee should pick up in a set amount of time.

Further on in the text is a section on a Field Training Officer (FTO) Program. In this section, the training is based on a formalized on-the-job training effort with three phases of training. Using the standard 90-day probationary period as a basis, the first month is developed with the trainer demonstrating the skills necessary for the job, with the trainee shadowing the trainer to learn the position. The second section is where the trainee performs the functions repeatedly with the trainer supervising and giving tips and corrections. The final month is proving mastery of the performance by the trainee teaching the skills back to the trainer, with the trainer asking pointed questions, such as which policy is this task describing. During the entirety of the FTO program, the trainer evaluates the trainee for attitude, wearing the uniform, customer service, and other soft skills.

Firearms training, marksmanship and qualifications, handcuffing, conducting investigations, first aid/CPR/AED, and self-defense have their own set of skills and performance objectives that require the trainer to be knowledgeable about the testing procedures and what is considered passable. Being a good marksman while having poor weapons retention or safe drawing skills may require additional training or failure.

Develop and Describe the Knowledge or Skills to be Tested

So, why test? Is the material imparted in the course so important that the student is tested to ensure the information is retained long enough to take the test? Is that period of retention all that is needed by your organization? Assuming that your security department training is critical to ensuring all are educated to a standard that the organization subscribes to, then I would also assume testing has relevance and time to develop a method to check the students' attention and motivation to retain the material is also important.

The next question is do you care about what grade the student receives after taking the test? What grade is considered passing to the course developer, your standard, and the organizational needs? If your organization has spent the resources to develop the courseware, is not all the information in the course worthy of being tested, and should the student pass with a 100% completion grade? Answering all the questions correctly may not be reasonable depending on the complexity of the concepts, student's ability, or motivation. So, what is a passing grade? What if the student fails – can they retake the course? What will your organization do with the grade?

In today's litigious society and risk avoidance through adhering to due diligence, if you determine that 75% is passing and the student gets 75%, then in court, you may be questioned why 75% was considered passing and not 76% or higher. Defending what is considered a passing score may be necessary. In training skills-based topics and their testing such as marksmanship, CPR/first aid/AED, what frequency of re-training and qualification do you subscribe to, yes you may be questioned, and should the students' scores get better with continuous training?

Testing is not supposed to be subjective. Which information is testable is identified when developing the course objectives, terminal objectives, and enabling objectives. Topics that are important to be tested are a function of the course development. Which topics are critical and should be tested, as well as what is considered a passing score must be designed into the development of the course.

Create a Specification for Testing

Creating a specification for the testing of both knowledge and skills topics is pretty simple. Start by describing the purpose of the test. Identify what topics are to be tested, who will be taking the test, and whether the testing is criterion-based or possibly norm-referencing.

Criterion-Based

This will probably be the most commonly used testing by readers of this text; however, know that in criterion-based testing "absolute score interpretation is the primary interest" (American Educational Research Association, 2014). In other words, when the test taker is being asked questions for the training topic and whether the questions are answered correctly or incorrectly, the testing only concerns whether the test taker got the answer correct.

Norm-Reference Based

"Relative score interpretations are the primary interest" (American Educational Research Association, 2014). This type of testing is typically when the test giver is trying to determine where the test takers rank among a specified group or demographic (e.g., age, grade, and job classification).

Additional information in determining the purpose of the test can be based on the number of questions to be asked, the type or question format, the length of the test, how the test will be administered, the allowed time for the test, and any instructions for the test administrator.

If the test is to be for a skill, the test administrator should have specific instructions to ensure the testing is unbiased and that each test taker is given an equal chance of success. Should a test administrator omit directions as to how the test will be given or what is expected of the test taker, the test taker is placed at a disadvantage.

If your security training is intended to conform to a municipal requirement, then verify that testing and qualifications also conform to that requirement. If this is your intent, in the testing specification document, the municipal requirement should be cited.

Draft Potential Test Items and How They Will Be Scored

After conducting the task analysis and while developing the LTG, you should consider how every critical topic can be tested, the best testing format for each topic, and if the topic is important enough to have a test question. Not all sub-topics may be testable, yet they are still important to describe, define, or assist in the student's comprehension. If explaining the difference between crimes against a person and property crimes, the students may ask many "what if" questions to assist in their understanding. You may see fit to include some of these in your course to add depth to the student's understanding of a topic, though not all examples will be testable for your organizational needs. Knowing the difference between property crimes and crimes against a person is all the student needs to understand.

Skills testing is more complicated. Determining if the skill was performed adequately, in an acceptable time, or in accordance with a checklist, or stated objective. Therefore, defining the test for skills testing will require additional information for the specification.

Adequately or satisfactorily performing the skill must start with a set of criteria. List the purpose of the skill and the set of criteria within which the skill will be tested. The criteria you select must be able to be replicated during future classes. For example, in marksmanship, a standard is that the shooter being tested will stand a set distance from a static target which is firmly fixed to a stand with the center-weighted target at an elevation of five feet or less than two meters from the ground. The shooter with a holstered, unloaded pistol, and two magazines containing five rounds will safely load and make ready upon the command and then completely re-holster. Upon the command, the shooter will draw from the fastened holster, fire five rounds with their strong hand only (one-handed), reload and fire five rounds with their weak hand (one-handed), and then safely re-holster an empty weapon.

I left out several criteria, such as hitting the center of the target, and how many seconds the tested student has to complete the line of fire. The above example is not a marksmanship course, it only gives the necessary details to ensure the person being tested is given all the requirements to be successful in the testing exercise.

NOTE:
Due to the legal system and the potential for being questioned as to your testing and grading standards, I have found departments do not maintain the actual test scores. They only record that the student passed or failed the test or skill. Something to consider and to discuss with your legal department.

Conduct and Review Pilot Tests and Evaluate the Quality of the Test Items and Questions

The more complex your courses are, the more important you will find the need to review the testing appliance. Most of us have found that following a course and taking the test, the class all missed the same question, though we taught the answer, or the class found a question on a test that was never discussed in the course, or a question was poorly written and was not understood by the class. All of these are reasons to review the testing you are suggesting the students take and pass.

ASIS International has always been concerned about its certification testing construct. For this reason, ASIS strives to follow best practices for exam development. All four ASIS Certifications have had third-party validation of these practices and are accredited to the International Standard for "Conformity Assessment for Personnel Certification Body" (ISO/IEC 17024-2012). These best practices ensure that each phase of the test development process bolsters the validity of the respective certification program. This includes providing clear and accurate information about the design of each exam and that policies are applied equitably to all applicants and candidates. For example, test takers know in advance how many questions will be on each exam. Additionally, each Body of Knowledge deemed necessary for mastery or essential knowledge for the certification includes what domain of practice and what percentage of exam items for each domain will be included. ASIS International certification examinations are administered to candidates via a computer-based testing system, which randomly orders the questions presented so that no two test takers will see the same questions in the same order.

NOTE:
After attaining my Physical Security Professional (PSP) certification from ASIS International, I assisted in vetting the question batteries by taking four PSP certifications in one day, which included discussing each question for its usability. Yes, I was numb after that.

In skills testing, greater weight may be given to the criteria of the skill to be performed. Using the example of CPR certification testing, having the student perform CPR on a person instead of a mannequin, or under some austere environmental conditions has little value to the skill being performed. But in marksmanship, standing in front of a paper target on an indoor range, without moving, or shooting from behind cover may not be realistic testing for such a critical skill. Another example would be handcuffing a compliant assistant versus handcuffing a combatant. Consider realistic marksmanship or tactical marksmanship training for your staff.

As written above, many test questions can be taken directly from the course or lesson objectives. If the objective is that the student can define the term "transferred intent" then the question on the test can be "Define and give an example of Transferred Intent."

Other questioning techniques can include multiple choice, selecting from a list, fill-in-the-blank, matching, true or false, and multiple choice. Unless the lesson is on report writing, an essay question is not recommended as the results may be too subjective.

Multiple choice is a very common questioning technique. The student must choose from a set of potential answers. It allows the student to discern between similar answers, testing recall, analysis, and evaluation. Multiple-choice questions make it less likely that the student will guess the answer. The question or problem is to be matched with the most correct answer from the list.

- The question should not contain irrelevant information and the question should be meaningful. Using questions such as "Which of the following is false?" is not meaningful, nor does it contain relevant information to a subject, lesson, or topic.
- The question should not be worded in the negative. The following increases confusion "Which of the following statements is not correct regarding criminal intent?"

- In most cases, only one answer is correct with the other distractors being closely worded or similar items from the same lesson.
- A drawback to multiple choice is the development of distractors or alternative answers. Implausible answers, silly answers, or intentionally misspelled words are not proof that the student attained the course objectives.
- "All the above" or "None of the above" should not be used. Answers such as "A and C," or the like, are also not a true test of the student's comprehension.
- Alternatives should be presented in a logical order so that no bias is presented by the order.

Select from a list can easily be used when discussing several definitions or components. The student is given two lists, and they are to match an item in one list to an item in the other list. An example would be a list of components to a list of functions or a list of crimes to a list of their definitions.

Fill-in-the-blank should be used sparingly because the word that is critical enough to test must be specific. The student may not use a synonym or alternate word that the instructor may have used during the class to aid in understanding. There are situations where it can be used efficiently, such as when specifics are important to the definition. An example would be: Per the California Penal Code, a minor is a person under the age of _____.

True or False questions are generally easy to develop.

- True/False questions are known for the student's ability to guess the answer, which may allow a passing score without an understanding of the topic.
- Testing a negative may not be considered valid training. If the question deals with a specific time, degree, or method, developing the question in the negative is not conducive to the student retaining the information. In the example: "The sky is green. T/F." If the student answers correctly (False) then the student still may not know the color of the sky.

Matching questions are similar to selecting from a list. The required actions by the tested student are similar and recall is used to match a definition to a term, or function to the component.

Example:

Draw a line from the term on the left column to an example in the right column.

Robbery	*Death of a human with malice aforethought*
Murder	*Physically striking another*
Battery	*Attempting to strike another but not making contact*
Maiming	*Cutting off an ear*
Assault	*Using force or fear to take property from another*

If an essay question is to be used, the conditions for the essay need to be specific and documented so that the next class taking this course will get the exact same conditions for the essay question. Additionally, the instructor must also know exactly what components need to be found in the essay answer to determine the grading.

- If the essay question can have a value of greater than a point, then the instructor needs to be able to successfully grade the answer based on the criteria. For example, if one of the essay's answer criteria is the correct use of punctuation. How many points are taken off for misusing punctuation, five times or ten times?

COURSE EVALUATIONS

Regardless of how many times the course has been taught, the instructor has taught the course, or the length of the course, an evaluation is necessary.

- Instructors have bad days, audio-visual equipment fails, the classroom is imperfect, and the students may be of a different academic level than for whom the course was developed.
- Maybe the course was perfect and every student enjoyed the knowledge and skills delivered professionally by your instruction staff.
- The test was made easy because the instruction and student guide helped to comprehend the course objectives.

Okay, the course was probably not so perfect nor was it a failure, but there is always some part of the course that could be refined, updated, editorial changed, or the process modernized. Asking your staff their opinions of the course is proof that you want the courseware to be the best and that your staff's opinion assists in the continual curriculum development process.

73

The evaluation process should be somewhat of a formal instrument that asks the students for their opinion on the classroom, length of the course, breaks, academic level of the course, audiovisual devices and presentations, handouts, tests, test review, skills testing, explanation of the requirements to pass the course, and expectations during class participation.

Considering the diversity of your staff, you may want to add questions as to the students' experience with the subject before taking the course, their language skill level of the language in which the course was instructed, and the testing administered. Having this knowledge can justify their answers to the evaluation. It does not mitigate what can be construed as negative comments, but it can give cause for budgeting additional course development for other languages or the need to hire or promote a fluent person in that language to become an instructor.

All evaluations have merit even the forms filled out with little thought as to how the evaluations are handled. Discussing an evaluation comment with a student shows the importance of the course evaluations and the student's opinions taken by your department.

REFERENCE MATERIALS

Throughout this book, there will be comments regarding references from which you draw your course material. There are several reasons for doing more than just citing your reference materials.

- By maintaining copies of your references, it will allow students, instructors, and other professionals to utilize the references whether simply to refer to the cited passage or to conduct research for future projects.
- At higher academic levels, you may want your staff to participate in writings that will require more in-depth research than they are used to conducting. Having a reference library will assist in their growth and experience in projects that require research.
- In our litigious society, your teachings may be met with legal queries as to the basis of your training program. Should a single point of the course be questioned as to its veracity, having the reference used in hand will reduce anxiety.
- Developing a formal library of documents, text or standards can assist your department in self-education and collegiate coursework.

- Whether the reference material is in digital or physical form, retention, and simple labeling and cataloging will go a long way in easing the burden of locating the document for later use.
- Do not simply save a URL or webpage where you found a reference you cited for this project. URLs and webpages are moved, shuffled, and removed all the time. To find the URL you cited as a reference no longer exists is as good as it never existed. Print the whole document if you can or download it to a ".pdf" and save the file in a location with other reference documents.

REVISE, UPDATE, AND MODERNIZE

The above discussion dealt with the training materials typically developed for each course, including objectives, LTGs, student guides, testing materials, course evaluations, and reference library. During your efforts to develop the curriculum, there will be other documents required for budgeting, approval, and working documents such as the task analysis and testing specifications document.

In planning for the development of courseware, the writing of the curriculum components is the document most utilized during the teaching of courses or training of skills. To this point we discussed identifying the needs for training, what tasks your staff perform that require you to provide training, and then the components of the curriculum. The next reality is that all courses age with changes to policies, organizational movements, and new products provided by your organization.

Course aging is common as the processes and needs of the organization will continue to change. Making minor or major changes to courseware requires documentation as to what was changed and the date. Larger changes may require a new set of objectives and even approval from your management-level employees.

All course material that is affected by the changes needs to be modified, and the changes noted. With all the work you have done, you do not want to find that an instructor off-site is teaching from an old LTG.

Changes that are mandated by legal requirements are critical for obvious reasons. However, the key to keeping up with legal changes is maintaining an ear to the ground, by networking with the right people and organizations. When you do get word of a legal change, take no one's word for granted. Get a copy of the statute and have your legal department review and produce a synopsis of the effect it will have on your organization. If necessary, contact your risk insurance department so they are also aware of changes. Keep the lines of communication open between departments as due to their advanced networks, they may get word of a legal change before you.

Keep in mind that anything can be the cause of changes to your curriculum. From technology changes with complete system modifications to a software update or something as simple as a change in badging materials.

If your organization has an office that oversees policies and procedures, or if there is an in-house document control or change management department, you may find they have a standard for making changes to documents. If not, a change management form is relatively simple in form and function. The change management form will be a running log and should accompany the full course document.

If the course is extremely long or complicated, you may have a change form per document. One for the test, the topic guide, and so on.

For a course, a single change management form should include the following:

- Course title and date of the original course
- Change in number
- Date of change
- Document where the change was made:
  In this section, specifics as to what was changed should be documented.
  (Example – LTG 5.2, Enabling Objective 5.2.1 and Student Guide for the above Course, page 23, item 5.2.1.3)
- Description of the change:
  (Example – "replaced Crime with Tort")
- Who made the change and who approved the change?

SUMMARY

Developing the courseware for your training effort will take some time both in the research and the writing. Take heart in knowing that training your new staff members will bring them faster to a level to perform their tasks in the way and means of your organization. Also, know that the many hours of documentation will set you apart from your peers. Your courseware will also aid in the betterment of our profession and give your newly hired staff the realization that there is room for promotion and raises when the time comes.

Section II

Layered and Secondary Course Development

6

Entry-Level Training

INTRODUCTION

As a general process, all training efforts should be constant and continuous. New hire orientation, new procedures, security academy, CPR/first aid/automatic electronic defibrillator (AED), marksmanship and firearms, drug recognition, gang updates, cybersecurity, crime prevention through environmental design (CPTED), current industry issues, crisis management, and on and on. The cycle of training, as well as the topics, is constantly being updated, and change is ever-present. This is a good thing as your training department will stay busy and your training offering will not grow stale.

A starting point such as a facility orientation or an academy is vital to setting a new employee on the right foot toward a successful career as well as ensuring the employee knows the objectives of their new organization and the position for which they were hired.

New hire orientation can encompass a considerable number of subjects with human resources alone taking a chunk of time. But from experience, a complete security orientation has value in bringing the new employee into assistance and increasing a robust security program. A peer once said that the security department included all the organization's employees as they were all responsible for the security of the personnel, facility, and operation.

As security is the organization's rule-keeper, ensuring that new employees know the importance of the organization's security posture and key processes of daily operations, for which they are responsible, is

DOI: 10.4324/9781003292586-9

vital to keeping them from making security errors, such as walking out the wrong door at the beginning of their employment. Using the officer-friendly approach, briefing a new hire with a positive attitude gives assurance of working in an important organization and within a secure environment.

Each new hire should go through one or more days of new hire orientation in which several subjects are covered by security. If the new hire will be part of your security staff, their next step should be an orientation of the security department. What the new hire should expect is a defined list of what will be expected of them and what training they will soon receive. Setting the expectations at the beginning of their employment should demonstrate that the training curriculum of your department is positive and formally systemic.

In a large department's security orientation, when numerous security hires are brought on at the same time, a security academy can be started as necessary. If you work in a department that brings on new hires less frequently, an academy can wait until several hires are gathered to hold the course. However, withholding an academy also means that your new hire is less than fully beneficial to your department until they are trained.

Depending on the complexity of your organization and the security operation, a security academy can be anywhere from an 8-hour to a 40-hour curriculum. Based on the availability of schedules and instructors, the academy can be scheduled in several ways, like being broken up over days or a couple of hours per shift. An important factor to consider is whether the new hire will be fully functional without attending the complete academy. Having an employee carrying a weapon before they attend firearms training is wrong, but so is putting an officer behind the wheel of a patrol car if they have not attended your company's mandatory driving curriculum. And obviously, there are many other examples such as handcuffing, CPR, access control systems, system inspection, and more. Consider training that is required immediately so your new hire is at least somewhat functional if your operation allows it.

At a minimum, in keeping with the standard 90-day probationary period, or whatever probationary period your organization subscribes, the new hire completes the academy before the end of that period. If using an on-the-job training period (discussed in Section II, Chapter 7), that should also conclude at the 90-day probationary period end.

ACADEMY TRAINING PLAN

Below is an example of a training plan for a security academy. Your organizational needs will undoubtedly be different from this example. However, it does demonstrate the detail that the training schedule should include. For your organization, you may add a column to identify the instructor(s). A benefit of noting the estimated duration of the class is should an instructor need to reschedule; the class can be plugged into the academy where needed and when possible. Remember that in some cases flow of training is still important if the lessons are building toward a knowledge topic (Figure 6.1).

No matter how long your newly hired security candidate has been in the security field or any associated field such as military or law enforcement, there needs to be initial training with your organization. If the candidate is brand new to the security field, explain to them their new job, their primary roles, how you want them to react and the duties they will perform, your required level of customer service as well as the basics of the facility, site, posts, and key personnel. If they are coming from the military or previous law enforcement positions, then the reminder that they are no longer in those roles and that there are differences that they need to know and acknowledge, such as the legal differences between security and law enforcement.

Initial training can also be for all new hires at your organization or site. This is a good time to roll out the rules of this facility, when and where badges will be worn and when they should not be worn, escorting guests, what constitutes a guest, and access to protected or special areas, just to name a few. Another key topic is your organization's security protocols and the role these employees or badge holders have toward security. One way to explain their role is that every employee or person with unaided access to the area is responsible for the security of the site. Then, explain their role to observe and report anything that is out of the ordinary or out of protocol.

Initial Training for Security Personnel – Security Academy

The big question here is what knowledge do you need to impart to your new hire? There are requirements by most states or municipalities for training security personnel. These requirements should be the basic and minimum level of what you should train. State requirements vary widely, so ensure your initial training covers the requisite topics.

Module	Est. Time	Module Title
1st Day		
	60	Introduction
1.1.1	60	Private Security Officers and the Criminal Justice System
1.1.3	15	Crime and Loss Prevention
1.2.6	75	State and Local Laws
1.1.2	60	Information Sharing
5.1	45	Safeguarding Information: Proprietary and Confidential
4.1	30	Ingress and Egress Control
4.2	75	Access Control Systems
2nd Day		
2.1	45	Observation Techniques
2.2	15	Note Taking
2.3	60	Report Writing
1.2.3	15	Court Testimony
1.2.4	20	Incident Scene Preservation
1.2.1	30	Evidence and Evidence Handling
1.3.1	15	Ethics
1.3.2	15	Honesty
1.3.3	15	Personal Image
3.3	15	Customer Service and Public Relations
3.2	20	Verbal Communication Skills
3.1	10	Interpersonal Skills
15.0	20	Crisis Management
6.1	45	Critical Incident Response
6.2	20	Evacuation Process
3rd Day		
7.1	15	Hazards in the Workplace/Surroundings
7.2	15	Emergency Equipment Placement
7.3	65	Fire Prevention Skills
7.4	10	Hazardous Materials
7.5	20	Occupational Safety and Health Requirements
1.2.5	15	Equal Employment Opportunity (EEO) and Diversity
9.1	15	Company Orientation and Policies
9.2	25	Substance Abuse
9.3	25	Communications Modes
14.0	5	Procedures for First Aid, Cardiopulmonary Resuscitation, and Automatic External Defibrillators
11.0	15	Conflict Resolution Awareness
10.0	35	Workplace Violence
8.1	10	Job Assignment
8.2	45	Post Orders
1.2.2	45	Use of Force and Force Continuum

Figure 6.1 Class schedule example.

4th Day

	12.0	30	*Traffic Control and Parking Lot Security*
	13.0	30	*Crowd Control*
	16.0	15	*Labor Relations*
	2.4	20	*Patrol Procedures*
		385	*Site Orientation*

5th Day

	17.0	240	*Oleoresin Capsicum Aerosol Training - Certification Course*
	18.0	240	*Practical And Tactical Handcuffing - Certification Course*

Figure 6.1   (*continued*)

Security Industry Standards

There are other studies, standards, and certifications that have identified initial training criteria. In the recent 2023, "Security Officers and Patrol Services Competency Model" developed by the International Foundation of Security Officers for the United States Department of Labor, using Maslow's hierarchy pyramid design, near the bottom of the pyramid is the Academic Competencies. These same academic competencies were also included in the 1993 University of Phoenix and ASIS Foundation report "Enterprise Security Risks and Workforce Competencies – Findings From an Industry Roundtable on Security Talent Development" and in the 2020 United States Department of Labor "Enterprise Security Competency Model."

Understandably, these are not solely collegiate requirements, they are simply competencies that are required for higher development. They include:

- *Security Fundamentals* – Understand and can apply basic security principles to the security of the enterprise or a specific structure, system, or process.
- *Business Foundations* – Understand basic business principles, trends, and economics.
- *Critical and Analytical Thinking* – Using logic, reasoning, and analysis to address problems.
- *Communications* – Giving full attention to what others are saying, and communicating in English (or other requisite language) well enough to be understood by others.

- *Reading and Writing* – Understanding written sentences and paragraphs in work-related documents. Using standard English (or other requisite language) to compile information and prepare written reports.
- *STEM (Science, Technology, Engineering, and Mathematics) Literacy* – Understand and apply science, technology, engineering, and mathematics to work within individual roles and responsibilities and in collaborating with allied workers.

In the 2004 "Private Security Officer (PSO) Selection and Training Guideline" (ASIS GDL PSO 11 2004) produced by ASIS International, and an updated version produced in 2019 (ASIS PSO-2019) the following essential topics for both proprietary and contract security officers are recommended. The training covers 48 hours and can be given in lectures, computer-based, or self-study. Regardless of the method of training, testing is required to ensure understanding and retention of the information. The guideline also recommends that annual refresher training be given to officers based on the facility, role, and needs.

Training Topics

- Nature and role of private security officers
  - Security awareness
    - Physical Security Officer and the Criminal Justice System, Information Sharing, Crime and Loss Prevention, Criminal and Civil laws
  - Legal aspects of private security
    - Powers of arrest, evidence and evidence handling, use of force, court testimony, incident scene preservation, equal employment opportunity and diversity, state and local laws, individuals' rights of privacy
  - Security officer conduct
    - Ethics, honesty, professional image
- Observation and incident reporting
  - Observation techniques, note taking, report writing, patrol techniques
- Patrol vehicle operations
- Physical and cybersecurity measures
- Interview techniques

- Principles of communications
  - Interpersonal skills, verbal communication skills, customer service and public relations, media interaction
- Control center operations
- Containment, search, and detention
- Principles of access control and visitor management
  - Ingress and egress control procedures, electronic security systems
- Principals of safeguarding information
  - Proprietary and confidential
- Emergency response procedures
  - Critical incident response, evacuation processes
- Processing of information and complaints
- Public safety/private security liaisons
  - Training in support of local law enforcement
- Life safety awareness
  - Safety hazards, emergency equipment, fire prevention skills, hazardous materials, OSHA-related training
- Job assignment and post orders
- Employer orientation and policies
  - Substance abuse, communication modes, mission, and values
- Workplace violence
- Equipment and materials management and controls
- Screening operations
- Gender and cultural issues and respect for the local population
- De-escalation and conflict resolution
- Traffic control and parking lot safety
- Crowd control
- First aid/CPR/AED
- Crisis management
- Labor relations

Looking at another recently published text on security, the following list of topics was recommended in the book *The Professional Protection Officer*, Second Edition.

- The role of the security officer
- Legal aspects of private security
- Use of force
- Note taking and report writing
- Court testimony

- Conduct and appearance
- Interpersonal communication skills
- Ethics
- Access control procedures
- Emergency response procedures
- Life safety procedures
- Patrol operations
- Intrusion detection and response
- Workplace violence response procedures
- First aid, advanced first aid, CPR, and AED

These are excellent starting places to identify what topics you may want for your organization and to determine what is needed for the initial training of new hires in security. The next critical listing of security training needs should come from the municipalities that govern the licensing of security personnel in your area. As written above, this is regardless of your team coming under their jurisdiction. If the state in which your organization operates requires that your new hires learn about three-legged purple zebras, then that should be included in your curriculum. Now obviously, the example is tongue in cheek, but the reality is that if every new security officer in the state is taught something, then regardless of whether it applies to your staff's operations, or not, it must be addressed in the training.

The main reason for including all topics from the municipal requirements is due diligence. Should your training ever be brought under that magnifying glass of a legal review, it ensures that your training, at a minimum, covers the areas required by the state to show deference to the municipal requirements. Municipal requirements will probably not be far from what your officers need. If you have a proprietary force and the municipality has legal requirements for a contractual force officer, it is good for your staff to know the differences.

Define the Need

At this point, you should be able to document a cogent need for the initial training of your newly hired security officers. To name a few needs: industry standards, municipal requirements, and the specific needs of your organizational security

Conduct a Task Analysis

Above are excellent lists of training needs as identified by our industry. The next step for your curriculum development is to watch your current staff for at least a week and document all the tasks that they are required to perform in that period.

Since you are conducting this exercise, I would also recommend that you collect as much data as possible including:

- Frequency of the task (how many times a shift is a task performed?)
- Time of the day (are there certain tasks that take place only at a specific time of day or shift?)
- How long is your officer assigned to this task? How many officers are required for the task?
- Does the task require supervision? Is a supervisor or managerial input required?
- Are there associated tasks, such as a phone call which can be one task, and the request for special access on that call another?

The gathering of this data will help determine when the training is given. Is the task considered elementary or intermediate in the scope of your staff's day-to-day?

NOTE:
Statistics can be a big help in your organization, therefore in past positions, I had the command center operators keep a running log of everything, then made a tally for ease of some tasks such as phone calls. Once, when budgets were being cut, I used my statistics to ask which task should be removed from security's responsibilities. Our budget went untouched. It is often that management forgets all the tasks your staff perform. Do not be shy in reminding them.

As this training effort will be considerable in length and the number of topics, to assist in the task analysis, a gap analysis may be helpful to determine where your current training offering sits and where it needs to be expanded (Figure 6.2).

Using the above chart, enter any additional duties that your staff conducts, and check the boxes that apply as these are the topics that will need to be included in your curriculum. You may also want to add a column of what training must be received at the beginning and before

	1	2	3	4	5	Organizational Needs	Priority
Leadership							
Security Fundamentals	X	X	X	X	X		
- Apply Basic Security Principles	X	X	X	X	X		
Business Foundations	X	X	X				
- Understand basic business principles	X	X	X				
- Business trends	X	X	X				
- Business Economics	X	X	X				
Critical and Analytical Thinking	X	X	X				
- Logic	X	X	X				
- reasoning	X	X	X				
- analyze	X	X	X				
Communications	X	X	X	X	X		
- Listening	X	X	X	X	X		
Reading	X	X	X				
- Understands written sentences and paragraphs	X	X	X				
Writing	X	X	X	X			
- Compile information and prepare reports	X	X	X	X			
STEM Literacy	X	X	X				
- apply STEM in security roles	X	X	X				
- apply STEM in collaborating with others	X	X	X				
Nature and Role of Private Security Officers				X			
- Security Awareness				X			
- PSO and the Criminal Justice System				X			
- Information Sharing				X			
- Crimes and Loss Prevention				X			
- Crimes and Civil Laws				X			

Figure 6.2   Task analysis matrix.

Legal Aspects of Private Security				X	X	
- Powers to Arrest				X	X	
- Evidence and Evidence Handling				X		
- Use of Force				X	X	
- Court Testimony				X	X	
- Incident Scene Preservation				X		
- EEOC and Diversity				X		
- State and Local Laws				X		
- Individual Rights of Privacy				X		
Security Officer Conduct				X	X	
- Ethics, Honesty				X	X	
- Professional Image				X	X	
Observation and Incident Reporting				X	X	
- Observation Techniques				X		
- Note Taking and Report Writing				X	X	
- Patrol Techniques				X	X	
Patrol Vehicle Operations				X	X	
Physical and Cyber Security Measures				X		
Interview Techniques				X		
Principles of Communications				X	X	
- Interpersonal Skills				X	X	
- Verbal Communication Skills				X	X	
- Customer Service				X		
- Public Relations				X		
- Media Interaction				X		
Control Center Operations				X		

Figure 6.2 *(continued)*

Containment, Search, and Detention		.		X			
Principles of Access Control and Visitor Management				X	X		
- Ingress and Egress Control Procedures				X	X		
- Electronic Security Systems				X			
Principles of Safeguarding Information				X			
- Proprietary and Confidential				X			
Emergency Response Procedures				X	X		
- Critical Incident Response				X	X		
- Evacuation Processes				X	X		
Processing of Information and Complaints				X			
Public Safety / Private Security Liaison				X			
- Training to support local law enforcement				X			
Life Safety Awareness				X	X		
- Safety Hazards				X			
- Emergency Equipment				X			
- Fire Prevention Skills				X			
- Hazardous Materials				X			
- OSHA Related Training				X			
Job Assignment and Post Orders				X			
Employer Orientation and Policies				X			
- Substance Abuse				X			
- Communication Modes				X			
- Mission and Values				X			
Workplace Violence				X	X		
Equipment and materials management and controls				X			
Screening Operations				X			

Figure 6.2   (*continued*)

Gender and Cultural Issues				X			
- Respect for the local population				X			
De-escalation and Conflict Resolution				X			
Traffic Control and Parking Lot Safety				X			
Crowd Control				X			
First Aid / CPR / AED				X	X		
Crisis Management				X			
Labor Relations				X			

Key to Source of Information in the Above Matrix:

1	2023 "Security Officers and Patrol Services Competency Model" developed by the IFPO for the United States Department of Labor
2	2020 United States Department of Labor "Enterprise Security Competency Model"
3	1993 University of Phoenix and ASIS Foundation report "Enterprise Security Risks and Workforce Competencies
4	2004 and 2019 ASIS International "Private Security Officer Selection and Training Guideline"
5	2023, "The Professional Protection Officer" Second Edition, Butterworth - Heinemann

Figure 6.2   (*continued*)

they start working as a security officer for your operation and which topics can be brought in shortly thereafter.

The next section will discuss a field training program, however, for this purpose, we will call the training On-the-Job (OJT) training. Not all tasks performed by your officers can be taught in a classroom, therefore, review the complete list, and identify which topics will require more than a lecture or other self-study format lesson. Or the topics that will require both lecture and OJT.

The final set of checks will be based on the priority set by your operations, which topics do you know your staff will need before working as a security officer for your organization? The list can be small or large, but regardless, which topics would you believe the candidate does not need on their first day in uniform? You can determine this better than anyone can because you are the one getting the phone call when a new hire on Post 23 will not let someone pass. After all, they have not been trained on the access control process and their frustration becomes less than customer service friendly to the vice president seated in the vehicle.

Determine the Training Form

Some security academies are lengthy and last more than a week. And, the topics require more than simple lectures due to the complexity, the introduction of software and hardware, potential marksmanship and weapons training, and the specialization of the sites to be protected.

The lecture has been the most common form of training since kindergarten, but lectures can also be delivered by video, or enhanced with computer programming to introduce short quizzes to ensure understanding. The use of lecture is generally the simplest delivery method but fulfilling a complete academy class may not be a reality as replacing or bringing on new personnel to your staff typically occurs one or two at a time. Conducting an academy lecture across multiple sites using video teaming software is helpful as there are still interactions between the instructor and students and student-to-student. Video teaming offers the ability to interject comments or questions posed by one student that can increase understanding or cause questions by others requiring the instructor to stay on the topic long enough to ensure understanding.

A time and cost-saving method is to conduct the lecture while the instructor is being videoed. There are technical nuances that the curriculum developer will need to consider, such as timing and breaks, as well as the presenter may need multiple takes on a few classes. If done well, the next new hire can watch a video and bring any questions to their supervisor at the end of the video, then take a short quiz to ensure the student paid attention well enough to retain the information.

All lectures can easily be sat through without the student paying attention or lacking any understanding of the materials. Therefore, testing throughout the course can be used to gauge both attention and comprehension with an immediate correction to prevent a failed understanding which would stop the new hire from progressing to the next topic.

Another form of training for elementary studies in your academy, such as criminal law, civil law, roles of security, and others is computer-based training (CBT). CBT has been around for decades and has become easier for the authoring of courseware. Using CBT typically takes fewer work hours for the supervisor or trainer, but it does not minimize time for the person receiving the training. The person responsible for authoring the courseware will need to learn the software and then develop the curriculum into the authorizing system.

There are plenty of positives in using CBT, time savings for the trainer, usable and available at any time, use as refresher training, and consistent training of the subjects. However, the negatives are over-simplistic graphics, bulleted topics instead of writing full statements, and teaching the test.

- Over-simplistic graphics tend to have a cartoonish look and not the professional, polished look of your organization. The alternative is budgeting for a graphic artist to help produce your training segments following your organization's parameters.
- Training topics cannot be relegated to bullet items on a slide. In producing a presentation, bullet points are used to introduce or list topics which are then discussed at greater length. Bullet items by themselves are not training discussions. Consequently, the slides produced for CBT authoring need to be more complex and complete to ensure the topic is discussed and covered completely.
- When coming up with test questions, it is too easy to take the question directly out of the lesson provided in the CBT. Therefore, the occurrence of teaching the test is too common. Some questions, such as definitions, roles of security, or assigning priorities that when developing questions, it is too easily taken directly from the previous text. So as not to teach the test, using multiple choice, matching term to definition, or assigning priorities from a list requires the student to use more than simple memorization to correctly answer the question.

Lastly, one drawback identified by several users of CBT is the fear or unfamiliarity with computer use by the students. In current times, this may seem uncharacteristic but it does happen. Depending on your security operation and the need for your personnel to use computers daily, if there is hesitation or lack of familiarity when using computers to conduct the training, this may be a red flag for continued employment.

Using multiple training forms is an excellent method of keeping the coursework a little more exciting for the student. If the academy cadet does not know how the next course will be given, it can create some enthusiasm and cause a change in the dynamics of the class. In a lecture, a new hire may not understand a concept but is afraid to bring up the problem as the rest of the class is made up of veteran security officers, but in a CBT or video format, the reluctant new hire may be willing to ask for clarification without the peer-pressure stopping the student's actions.

Select the method of training delivery that best fits your personnel, their academic level, the tasks to be performed, and the needs and availability of your organization.

Develop Objectives

As stated before, this course will probably be several days of training and the course a conglomerate of topics. The course objective should be a broad brushstroke statement that identifies the purpose of the course and some of the major topics. Then as the course is broken into lessons, each key lesson would have a topic-specific objective.

Use the "Observation and Incident Reporting" listed above as important topics to be taught during private security introductory lessons. And, the subtopics will include Observation Techniques, Note Taking, Report Writing, and Patrol Techniques. Therefore, in this example, there will be a course objective covering "Observation and Incident Reporting," with Enabling Objectives covering the sub-topics.

Example:

Course Objective: Security Officers at the organization will be required to write accurate and meaningful reports and take in-depth notes from their observations, actions, and statements made to them by witnesses and those involved in the incident. Therefore, the importance of being observant, taking usable notes, and writing in paragraph form with correct punctuation and English is critical to the position of security officer at this organization.

Enabling Objectives:

1. *Being observant is one of the two most critical tasks a security officer will perform. The student will demonstrate the Identify, Observe, and Understand (IOU) tactic in sharpening their observing skills by using the CBT time-based observation and then document items in a timed photograph or illustration. Similar illustrations will be used for testing the skills requiring 80% accuracy.*
2. *The student will be taught the importance of note taking, cataloging notes by date, time, and location, using a new note page per witness statement, sets of facts, and answering the questions of who, what, where, why, how, and when with the assistance of the company provided notebook pages. The student will be tested in a scenario-based event provided by the instructor.*

When grouping sub-topics from the task analysis and listing course subjects from the above list and your research, develop the teaching of the topics in a structured flow that is natural and builds upon the prior subjects. For instance, teaching report writing after criminal law to see if the student can use the elements of a crime in their report. Or, teaching report writing, before teaching company policies so the student can determine the correct action and reporting if an employee breaks protocol.

If the length of the course is a problem with getting your staff operational, consider which topics can stand on their own, yet still be a part of the New Hire training syllabus. First aid/CPR/AED training could be a good example of this as most organizations have to schedule an instructor or find a class for the trainee to attend. Setting a portion of the training aside for scheduling is only a problem if there is a chance the staff will need these necessary skills for their immediate employment.

There is a stipulation that for each topic that is taught at a later time, the staff member cannot be put in a role where the training is necessary for them to perform their job. Firearms, marksmanship, use of force, handcuffing, or even driving a patrol are examples of this condition. If the officer is not trained by your organization for these roles, then they cannot be expected to follow rules that have not been taught. Use of force for security is generally a legal matter, therefore training is a must, but using the example of driving a patrol vehicle, when can they use the light bar, when can they double park, can they block other vehicles, can the officer use the loudspeaker during hours of darkness near residential areas, can the patrol vehicle be taken to the local coffee shop to pick up a drink while on shift, and more questions exist.

Write the Course

Now that the objectives are written based on the task analysis and other research, it is time to write the course. The easiest way is to put the title of the course at the top of the page, then the course objective. Put the first Enabling Objective next and then start jotting down everything your staff member needs to know about that sub-topic in bullet points or an outline style. Then continue with the next subtopic.

Any analogy, story, or example that will assist the students in remembering and understanding the information is important and should be documented next to the associated sub-topic bullet point. A review of these examples and the entire course is required to ensure the drafted examples benefit the organization, its purpose, and its ethics. Additionally, as your organization may have more than one dedicated trainer, each person fulfilling the role should have their example or have a complete understanding of the example documented so that confusion is not injected into the topic.

Testing

Testing has two purposes, to ensure comprehension and to increase information retention. Throughout the course, you can develop into the course several questions to gauge understanding. One method is to ask a few questions at the end of each topic that can then be formalized into a written quiz with a few fill-in-the-blank statements, match the word to the definition, multiple choice, or true and false.

There are positives and negatives to developing test questions (see Chapter 10).

Taking a test is stressful for some students, so ensuring the test is not intended to cause the student to question their understanding. Questions need to be developed without double negatives or asking a question in a negative form.

Examples of bad questions:

Which of the following is not the correct way to patrol?

It is not okay to drive on the left side of the road. True/False

7

Field Training Officer (FTO)/ Field Training Program

INTRODUCTION

Anyone who has trained in law enforcement will remember that a majority of academy classes are more academic than operational. Academics in law enforcement and security are critical to career success, but they must be combined with an operational curriculum. In keeping with law enforcement conventional titles, the operational training is a Field Training Operation (FTO) program. Departments have initiated FTO programs of all sorts and styles. This book will cover the use of the FTO program to encompass the operational aspects of the position as well as formalizing the probationary period.

As with all training, the information to be covered in the FTO program needs to meet the same standards as the academy and other courses you plan to offer, in that a task analysis must be completed, and objectives formalized. The task analysis performed for your entry-level training should be documented well enough to allow for the operational performance topics to be identified.

Using the FTO program to cover the probationary period can encompass more than just training by offering weekly reviews to include uniform, behavior, attitude, performance, and other standard issues covered during probation. I have found that most probationary periods are less formalized, therefore having one that requires a weekly performance review will properly document the new hire's performance

DOI: 10.4324/9781003292586-10

and measure that performance as acceptable or lacking. The form should also be used for corrective actions and developmental discussions. Hopefully, during the first 90 days, the new officer will continue to do better and be more of an asset, or the reports can be used to justify dismissal for failure to pass the probation.

Using the FTO program to instruct the new hire in operational methods and the specific way your organization does common tasks is critical to ensuring your company and its security staff provide consistent service.

One option to formalize the program to a higher degree is to break the 90 days into three 30-day periods. In the first period, the new hire must shadow a senior officer and be shown all aspects of the job. In the second period, the new hire performs all the standard tasks as shown by the senior officer in the first 30 days, with the senior officer offering suggestions and corrections along the way. This will include calling out repeated errors, offering corrective action, and validating correct behavior. In the last 30-day period, the new hire will teach the necessary skills back to the senior officer, with the senior officer asking questions that require the new hire to provide policy and procedural references, offer corrective actions to the senior officer, and thereby learning through teaching.

This teaching/training tactic may be familiar as it is typically coined, "see one, do one, teach one" and is used in many branches of the military, the medical fields, throughout industry, and in vocational settings.

If an academy class is scheduled within the FTO program, the program should allow for adequate time for both to occur simultaneously. Some police departments have engaged in a more advanced training setup where the academy and field mentoring occur throughout the new officers' training. By breaking up the academy with periods of field training it assists with enforcing skill sets, such as verbal negotiations and investigative techniques.

The FTO program approach supersedes the old on-the-job training (OJT). Superseded in that OJT typically requires the new hire to follow another employee around and determine their new job on that basis. You may remember being on OJT and being a gopher for the senior employee without any metrics to learn skills. The FTO program is a structured and well-developed program covering the majority of critical tasks and potential events the new employee may encounter.

Remember that the critical issue of training is to ensure a new hire is not placed in a position requiring skills or knowledge that has yet to be trained, such as carrying a firearm or evidence collection.

GETTING STARTED

As in any training development, the subsequent steps need to be followed and documented.

- Define the need
- Conduct a task analysis
- Develop objectives
- Write the curriculum
- Determine and develop testing

When a new hire is being taught, there typically is academic learning and then there is using what was taught in real life. As a child, we are taught how to add and subtract, and later how to balance our bank accounts. So, taking the basics of mathematics and putting them to use in the real world. The FTO program is similar but has a greater additional training value. You should know that most of what security personnel do and how those tasks are performed may not be teachable in the classroom. The FTO program should include the following:

- How the employee is to react to customer requests, requests for out-of-the-ordinary permission, during an emergency, during crises, even as to how the phone is to be answered or what radio codes are used.
- If uniform appearance or grooming standards are important, these should be included in the FTO program and its testing parameters.
- What to do in all cases to include the manner and attitude of the officer during that interaction. Therefore, tact, bearing, and attitude should be included in the FTO curriculum and testing.

While seated in the academy classroom, the basics of criminal law, the elements of crime, the primary duties of the new hire, the state and/or municipal required training, and specifics of the software to be used and how that software interacts with security systems will be taught, just to name a few topics of the formal academy.

The training provided within the formalized FTO will put those topics into real-life situations.

- How criminal law and elements of a crime are identified at the scene of an incident to make a radio call or notification to law enforcement and management.

- Adding a newly badged employee to the access control system for the correct approved level of access, where that access approval comes from, and what the different access levels represent.
- Which doors are unlocked with their badge, what biometrics do, and how they are stored and recorded as well as the enrollment process and orientation.
- How video is reviewed when something questionable is seen on a monitor and requires immediate review.

THE PROBATIONARY PERIOD

Most companies with which I am familiar have a probationary period for new hires. This period allows supervisors to determine if the new hire can perform the job and can grow in the position to be a valuable employee to the organization.

The FTO program can be performed within the probationary phase and add formality to the period. After an initial orientation for new security personnel, initiation into the FTO program starts the training period. A senior security person should be assigned as a Field Training Officer to the new hire.

Depending on the complexities of the security operation for which you are developing training, one recommendation is to fit the majority of the FTO program within the probationary period. If the probationary period at your organization is 90 days, then adding each of the "see one, do one, teach one" processes to a thirty-day window will allow for complete maturation of the process which requires training.

An important component of the FTO program and any probationary period is performance reviews. Waiting until the end of the 90 days to write a performance review is sadly inappropriate. Hence, the FTO program includes the need to evaluate the new hire on a weekly or at least a more periodic basis. Security is about enforcing rules, the training and skills required of new hire security personnel should be kept and managed similarly. (See Figure 7.1 for weekly performance review.)

Back to the "see one, do one, teach one" – it should be obvious that giving each step 30 days is a good start. However, allocating more time to "see one, do one" may be required based on your organization's complexity.

Probationary - FTO Program
Security Officer Weekly Evaluation

Employee Information		

Employee Name:	Date of Hire:	
Job Title: **Security Officer**	Job Code:	**S-1**
FTO:	Date:	
	Academy	
Review Period: **Week** *(circle one)*	Graduate:	**Yes** **No**
1 / 2 / 3 / 4 / 5 / 6 / 7 / 8 / 9 / 10 / 11 / 12		

Evaluation		

Check the box - *Use this rating key for the*
following evaluation:
*0 = **No:** Does not perform required tasks. Requires*
constant supervision.
*1 = **Meets:** Meets basic requirements. Tasks are completed*
on time.
*2 = **Exceeds:** Goes above and beyond*
expectations.

	Exceeds	Meets	No
Shows good judgment	··	··	··
Makes good decisions	··	··	··
Tact	··	··	··
Integrity	··	··	··
Dedication to job	··	··	··
Takes initiative in the absence of orders	··	··	··
Shows enthusiasm when conducting duties	··	··	··
Bearing (militarily carries themselves)	··	··	··
Good knowledge of procedures	··	··	··
Understand concepts of procedures and post-orders	··	··	··
Understands basic security concepts	··	··	··
Seeks self-improvement	··	··	··
Tactically proficient	··	··	··
Seeks responsibility	··	··	··
Takes responsibility for actions	··	··	··
Communicates clearly and effectively	··	··	··
Gives clear and concise orders	··	··	··
Follows orders without challenging the order	··	··	··
Provides good customer service	··	··	··

Figure 7.1   Example weekly evaluation.

101

Accomplishes assigned tasks (including training
assignments)

Ability to multi-task

Command presence

Quickly responds to events or directives

	Yes	No

Attendance

Meets attendance requirements

Ready for work on time and in uniform before the
start of the shift

Appearance	Yes	No
Is uniform clean and pressed?		
Are boots shined?		
Is the overall appearance of the uniform neat?		
Is hair neat and groomed?		
Is facial hair neat and groomed?		

FTO Observations

Security Officer Comments
(If no comments, write NONE in the space below.)

Verification of Review

By signing this form, you confirm that you have discussed this review in detail with your FTO.

_____

Security Officer Signature   *Date*

_____

FTO Signature   *Date*

Figure 7.1   (*continued*)

During these 90 days, an academy class can be convened and the new hire be sent to the academy. Unless the security organization is large enough to have a constant group of new hires to allow for a more structured security academy calendar, an academy class can convene as needed based on the hiring of new employees (see Security Academy, Chapter 10).

NOTE:

- The person who will be conducting the training or the Field Training Officer, needs to undergo training befitting the role. The FTO should have in-depth knowledge and operational experience in any task that the FTO is responsible for ensuring is conducted correctly. The selection for this position should also include an assessment of the candidate's enthusiasm for the product and service that security provides, a penchant for being considerate and patient in the training process, the ability to be fair and unbiased when evaluating others, and be a model to the trainee.
- The FTO's training should not be informal. Formalizing the training received by the staff member and having a competent trainer for new employees is a vital component and should not be taken lightly. A few hours of lecture on the purpose and legalities of evaluating a subordinate is essential knowing that the candidate's poor performance could mean their loss of employment. It should also include a run-through of the FTO items, and the FTO explaining the sections and policies that cover them.
- Developing a formal curriculum should be in keeping with other courses within your department's training measures. This is how we train our staff and this is how we train those that will be training our staff.
- The FTO's training can be done a few hours a day one-on-one with a manager, alleviating additional man-hours.

DEFINE THE NEED

Does your organization need a Field Training Program (FTP) to ensure the security staff is well-trained to perform the job within the guidelines of the job description?

What skills and verified performance can be gained by a FTP? Defining the need starts here, with a list of suggestions.

- Roles of the program, the Field Training Officer, and the new hire
- Access control protocol
- Surveillance
- Role of customers
- Role of vendors
- Customer service – software and database
- Policies, procedures, post orders, their value, and the enforcement role of security and the organization
- Report writing, basics, and elements of the crime or event
- Evidence handling, marking, and association in the report
- Patrols including on foot, in a vehicle, using all your senses, recognizing, and acting on unusual changes, public interactions
- Conducting escorts and interacting with guests being escorted
- Fire system panels, pumps, pressure gauges, risers, sprinkler heads, smoke/heat detectors and the role of their inspection during patrol, and what to do during a system event
- Conducting investigations, interviewing personnel, and gathering information. Documenting information with notes, following investigative leads, and recalling observations
- Incident scene preservation and protection
- Operational security incidents

CONDUCT A TASK ANALYSIS

When it comes to the FTP, just about every routine and event that could turn into a crisis has tasks that the security employee will partake in and should be included in the training. However, to conduct the task analysis have your supervisors document every task a group of security employees performs in a week, then rate the importance of the tasks based on criticality and importance.

Example:

- Answering the phone may not be considered critical to some but information being received by security on any call can be important.

So, the tasks have been identified, and the criticality assigned, now determine if it can be taught in the academy, in the field, or both. If the security academy is scheduled a month after the new hire starts, then the importance of training the common events should be moved forward.

DEVELOP OBJECTIVES

By now you probably have a good feel for why the training is necessary. Using the input from the task analysis develop a cogent set of objectives for the training event. In the case discussed above, a terminal objective for the whole program and then enabling objectives should be drafted to cover each 30 days.

WRITE THE CURRICULUM

After review of the task analysis, group the tasks into comprehensive piles, such as patrol procedures, fire prevention, and report writing. Itemize the tasks in a flow order where one seemingly may come before the other or in a series on which they build on each other. Now draft a statement covering each item that needs to be trained. If the task is to check doors while on foot patrol, the training may be to look for evidence of tool marks, is the door latched and secure, is there evidence of a door closure leaking fluid, is the door in need of repair or repainting due to wear, are applicable signs affixed and legible, and so on.

Document the training for each task in your organization's formal training documentation.

DEVELOP TESTING

For the FTP, testing is not a paper and pencil test, it is the new hire performing or explaining the task in accordance with your organization's applicable references, and in a manner that the FTO accepts. The main intent of all security training is that the whole team does every task with the same methodical precision, and in the same way allowing for no ambiguity or insecurity with your program.

SUMMARY

Security's day-to-day taskings are typically mundane and repetitive, and every once in a while, a special task or an incident occurs that requires the security employee to handle the event. Regardless of the daily or the special assignment, all possible scenarios should be considered to ensure the employee has received consistent training or is under direct supervision. Depending on the new hire, their experience, maturity, and education can allow for some to pick up the information quicker than others, but when consistency in the enforcement of policies and procedures, the effectiveness of the team approach to security, and management's need to rely upon security personnel to know how to do their job in accordance with the way the organization wants it done can only be trained through a program such as the FTP.

An integral part of this training is a senior trusted security employee to oversee and walk new hires through how your organization runs its security program and thereby accept the role of a trainer. The FTP has been tested and is used by most police departments in the United States to ensure employees are given OJT based on an instructional system development process.

To assist in understanding the FTP, please refer to the examples in Figure 7.2.

FIELD TRAINING OFFICER'S
SECURITY OFFICER'S MANUAL

FIELD TRAINING OFFICER   **SECURITY OFFICER**

Mission Statement – *The Security Department, in keeping with the expectations for professional security service, has established the Field Training Officer Program to:*

- *Prepare Probationary Security Officers to perform the essential duties of a Security Officer.*
- *Enhance the professionalism of the company through continuous quality improvement.*

Program Objectives –

- *To provide standardized probationary-level training for the Security Officer.*
- *To provide remedial training in those areas where deficiency is identified.*
- *To establish a system to ensure every probationary Security Officer receives the same training and their performance to that training is measured with the intent to succeed in all subjects.*
- *To work toward continuous quality improvement.*
- *To identify weaknesses or areas of improvement in the company's candidate hiring qualifications and Security Academy training.*

The Field Training Officer is a vital component to the training you will receive while going through your probationary period of 90 days.

Role of the Field Training Officer (FTO) *- The FTO is a Security Officer, Security Supervisor, or Security Manager who is responsible for your training. The FTO is a person to whom Security Management determined has complete knowledge of the tasks and information you will perform and need daily. The FTO is responsible to:*

- *Train the Probationary Security Officer in daily duties and essential functions of the position.*
- *Monitor the Probationary Security Officer through direct observation, radio traffic, and discussions with more senior Security Officers and other supervisory personnel.*
- *Maintain an instructor/mentor relationship with the Probationary Security Officer.*
- *Ensure the Probationary Security Officer completes all subjects listed in this manual.*
- *Provide proper reports of progress and the Manual's subject checklist, to include remediation training when necessary.*

Figure 7.2   Example Field Training Officer's manual.

- *Provide feedback to Security Management for changes, additions, and deletions to the Manual.*
- *Continue to provide and perform shift patrol duties.*
- *Notify Security Management of any issue that may affect the Probationary Security Officer's ability to complete the FTO Program and thereby complete his probationary period.*

A single FTO will be assigned to a Probationary Security Officer during the first 90 days, however, should the need arise; the FTO can be replaced with another FTO to complete the training period.

<u>Your Role</u> - As a Security Officer within the first 90 days of employment (probationary period) you are required to be trained and retain knowledge and skills that have been deemed important in the fulfillment of your position. Though you are responsible for the upkeep of this FTO Manual you will only make markings in it with your FTO's permission or at his/her direction. The FTO Manual is kept with you so you are fully aware of what information you need to successfully pass your probationary period. You are responsible to:

- *Participate in the FTO Program as an essential function of your job.*
- *Notify your FTO of any issues that may affect your ability to complete the FTO Program and thereby complete your probationary period.*
- *Maintain this Manual and all papers, notes, and assignments issued by your FTO.*
- *Notify your FTO and Supervisor of any period where you cannot be at work, such as military training, vacation, personal time off, etc.*

<u>The Manual</u> - This manual is divided into sections based on tasks and systems used within Security Command and is a part of the company's security operations and therefore make up some of the security protocols of the company.

In each section, there is a topic, and to the right of the topic, boxes are labeled Witness, Demonstrate, and Explain. This order of performance is based on the military style of "See One, Do One, Teach One". Each has a box for a date or dates when the task is accomplished, and a box for the FTO's initials when the task is completed to a level of perfection identified by the FTO.

*<u>See One</u> - **MUST BE ACCOMPLISHED WITHIN THE FIRST 30 DAYS OF EMPLOYMENT** - This section of the task is where the FTO will fully demonstrate and give direction of how a task is to be completed and pass on knowledge of the reasons and/or purpose for the subject.*

Date of Hire _____ Day 30 _____

Figure 7.2   *(continued)*

___

Do One - *MUST BE COMPLETED WITHIN THE FIRST 60 DAYS OF EMPLOYMENT* - *This section of the Tasks requires you to demonstrate the knowledge through skills thatthe tasks and knowledge require.*

Date of Hire _____ *Day 60* _____

Teach One - *MUST BE COMPLETED WITHIN THE FIRST 90 DAYS OF EMPLOYMENT* - *This section of the task is where you must explain, verbally, how to perform the task or knowledge with a complete explanation of the reason and/or purpose for the subject. You will be teaching your FTO how to complete the task with speed, and flawless accuracy.*

Date of Hire _____ *Day 90* _____

Disclaimer: - *The FTO Manual and all portions of security training are intended for internal use only. This manual should not be construed as a creation of a higherstandard, but only as a continuation of the training received by all Security Officers at the company.*

The term Probationary Security Officer is not a specific title but only a descriptor to identify the period of training that a new Security Officer attends.

ACCESS CONTROL (AC)

Access control is a matter of granting access based on identifying the person wishing access and identifying the rule set that goes with that person.

"Who are you?"

And

"Why should I let you in?"

To answer these questions, the company uses technology (Access Control System), protocol (Access Control Procedure), and personnel (you).

Protocol: *The company's protocol requires each department within the company and any customer to identify a Security Point of Contact (SPOC). Additional SPOCs can be named to assist in their operations since, at times, the SPOC may be unavailable. The SPOCs must tell the company's security management that they wish to have a representative from their department or company have access to the site and list any restrictions. Once received and verified, security management approves the access and either a badge is made or the representative is escorted to the space. The company never grants someone access without prior notification. The only exception is when a person badged for the facility brings someone in as a guest. Even then, we identify the person through an ID before issuing a badge.*

Figure 7.2 *(continued)*

The items listed under the AC topics have been identified and you will need to demonstrate adequate knowledge of the tasks associated with Access Control.

Security Academy Reference Materials:

4.0 Principles of Access Control (4.1 / 4.2)

8.0 Job Assignment and Post Orders

SURVEILLANCE / CCTV (CC)

Surveillance is a set of protocols combined with technical capabilities and your natural inquisitive instinct. For more than half a workday, the cameras remain in a fixed position which was chosen for the best scene to assist those in Security Command. These camera positions may change between working day and off-shift hours as, depending on the camera position, the threat may have changed. During times when there are few in the facility, the threat from a person within is minimized allowing security to be more watchful for outsider threats.

The protocol security uses to "watch" cameras is Identify – Observe – Understand (I-O-U). This easy-to-remember protocol allows for an observer to look for unusual issues, and observe them for a period until an understanding of the incident is identified. Simply moving a camera around has little use in conducting surveillance.

The company uses several surveillance systems and apparatuses. The company uses both fixed and pan/tilt/zoom (PTZ) capable cameras. The fixed cameras allow for an unmovable, ever-present video view of a location, such as a parking lot, door, or hallway. The PTZ-capable cameras allow for investigative capabilities and the following of moving objects, such as cars and people around and within the facilities. The company also uses a few systems to record the camera views.

The items listed under the CC topics have been identified and you will need to demonstrate adequate knowledge for the tasks associated with Surveillance and CCTV.

The company Security Academy Reference Materials:

2.1   Observation techniques

8.2   Post Orders

CUSTOMER INFORMATION DATABASE

The company uses a subscription-based, web-based application that contains customer information entered and used by the company in several departments. For example, contractual agreements, changes to those agreements, communications with the customer, and a list of contact information reside in the database. Specific to security, this is where the Security Points of Contact (SPOCs) are listed. You may find a similar list in other locations; however, this is the official listing: official because it is the master list and the list on which we rely. All other lists

Figure 7.2   *(continued)*

of SPOCs are derived from this official list and are therefore untrusted. I strongly recommend against making such lists within Security.

The company Security Academy Reference Materials:

3.2   *Customer Service*

4.1   *Ingress and Egress Control Procedures*

Other Reference Materials:

Database Instruction Guide - POI

POLICIES / PROCEDURES / PERIODS OF INSTRUCTION / POST ORDERS (PP)

In the security profession, one of the most critical documents is the Post Orders as it is what tells you your job and how to complete tasks that may not be necessary daily. The Post Orders derives its power from the Security Policy which is flowed down through Security Procedures. When procedures become complicated, a Period of Instruction (POI) is published to assist in your knowing how to perform tasks.

These documents are important to your professionalism, the security of the company, and even your position at the company.

Security Academy Reference Materials:

The Security Academy in its entirety

Other Reference Materials:

All Security Policies

All Security Procedures

All Security Periods of Instruction

Security Post Orders

COMPANY DATABASES

The Company Database is the internal web application that allows you access to information and where you will input data into various databases. The Company Database includes additional modules for all departments to use. The Company Database is a compendium of events that will occur, are occurring, or have taken place at the company.

The Incidents Module within the Company Database has two sections, Flagged Incidents, and a List of Incidents. Everything you do during your shift will be entered into the Incident Module to provide a searchable database. When entering an incident, such as when another Security Officer

Figure 7.2   *(continued)*

is issued keys, the incident remains open or "flagged" until the keys are returned. Therefore, the Flagged Incidents are those that require additional attention.

The Pass Down includes items with historical value such as a be-on-the-lookout (BOLO) subject or instructions on how to handle certain events.

The Customer Module is often used as a reference as it is your authentication to grant someone access to customer equipment. Failure to provide access has dire consequences, but granting access to someone without authorization is a terminating offense. Learn this module well.

The Customer List, Facility Code, and Key Chart modules are references for you to do your job. As customers are important, you do not need to know each customer and their employees, these are a sure way of locating a customer space and knowing how to enter the space. Both modules contain protected information for which you will learn the limits of releasing such information to a customer.

The Company Security Academy Reference Materials:

8.2   Post Orders

Other Reference Materials:

Customer Vendor Procedure

PATROL PROCEDURES (PA)

Patrol and security go hand in hand. A foot patrol is not just walking around. A camera patrol is not just moving the cameras. And a vehicle patrol is not just driving around.

All your senses are used when conducting patrols, feeling for humidity changes, smelling for odors, looking for unusual lights, hearing the high pitch of an alarm, and tasting the bile rise in your throat from the instinctive reaction when a procedure is not being followed.

As most FTOs will tell you when on patrol, you need to recognize change, view someone's actions for normalcy and compliance with policy, and distinguish unusual events from common daily activities. To identify these, you must first know what is common or normal and understand all of the company's procedures and policies

Security Academy Reference Materials:

The Security Academy in its entirety

Other Reference Materials:

Security Policies

Security Procedures

All Security Periods of Instruction

Security Post Orders

Figure 7.2   (continued)

FIRE SYSTEMS AND PREVENTION (FS)

Prevention of a fire or fire-related event is critical to the sustained performance of the company. Preventing fires may be easily understood, but fire-related events such as smoke, or the use of an extinguishing agent are just as devastating to the company, our industry, and our customers. Any such event can give the company an ill-perceived black eye. For the same reason, just the odor of smoke can cause problems. A release of a fire extinguishing agent is telltale to a real event. While an extinguisher does well at putting out fires, it also causes a mess and potentially costly damage to expensive equipment. Water is also deadly in our protected spaces with computer equipment, high voltage electrical current, and damage to equipment.

For the above reasons, proactive prevention of fires is the name of our game. Remove a fuel source from an environment and a fire cannot evolve. Combined with the deployment of smoke detection systems, the company can react to small events so they do not become large events.

Security Academy Reference Materials:

7.0 Fire Prevention and Hazardous Materials in the Workplace

Other Reference Materials:

Fire Safety Procedures

Fire Extinguisher Training POI

Fire Alarm Control / Fire Riser and Booster Panel POIs

INVESTIGATIONS (IN)

Not everyone is cut out to be an excellent investigator, but everyone can ask questions, document their statements and observations accurately, retrieve and protect evidence, and write a well-worded report.

Investigative skills start with a healthy inquisitive sense. When responding to a call you should know how to look for evidence, how to protect the scene and evidence, how to catalog the notifications to be given, and the actions to take. Once on the scene, do not allow yourself to see only the reported event. Look further to find associated actions, placement of equipment, and people present. Ask and document what everyone witnessed and where they were at the time of the incident. Think of what processes led to this event and what steps were omitted or changed to meet the needs at the time.

Photograph, video, measure, draw, list, write, and describe the event, scene, placement, and record the smallest item and observation for future needs. You may be asked to recall your actions

Figure 7.2 *(continued)*

113

and observations at a later date and in front of a judge. Write down everything and then keep it to protect yourself and the company.

Security Academy Reference Materials:

1.2.1 Evidence and Evidence Handling

1.2.4 Incident Scene Preservation

2.2 Note Taking

Other Reference Materials:

Report Writing Procedure

Figure 7.2   *(continued)*

8

Training That Requires Continuous Efforts

INTRODUCTION

Several subjects will require continuous and constant training. Due to either critical skills, perishable skills, or simply their litigious nature, these subjects require constant training as a risk reduction tactic.

Topics included in this section are as follows:

- Weapons.
  - Firearms
  - Electroshock or Conducted Energy Weapons
  - Baton and Impact Weapons
  - Chemical Sprays, Tear Gas, and Oleoresin Spray
- First Aid, CPR, and AED
- Handcuffing/Self-Defense
- Tactical Communication/De-escalation

NOTE:

The chapters in Section II of this book are meant to standalone meaning that each chapter can, in general, stand on its own topics. However, the requirements for curriculum development, task analysis, identifying needs, testing, and other subtopics may require the reader to return to another chapter in Section II for clarity.

DOI: 10.4324/9781003292586-11

WEAPONS

As a general rule of risk and security management, if your department personnel carry weapons, then important steps need to be followed when determining the initial training, and the amount and frequency of continued training. Just as a reminder, any item described or carried as a potential weapon requires training. This would include, but is not limited to, firearms, electroshock weapons, one of several forms of baton/striking weapon, tear gas, or oleoresin capsicum (OC) pepper spray, and less commonly, a knife.

Any weapon used should be taught from a position of practice, practical experience, and certification. Within your department, you may find that more than half of your staff have been trained on how to use firearms. Their previous training could come from military service, law enforcement employment, prior security experience, hunter safety classes, or personal family training. This variety of training causes a problem for your organization in that there may be too few similarities in the training and the training may not be specific to the weapons your organization provides or allows. Therefore, baseline training should be a requirement for all security staff who will be armed with weapons.

This text should not be considered or construed as legal advice. Please contact your legal team regarding the intricacies and ever-changing laws of providing weapons training.

FIREARMS AND MARKSMANSHIP TRAINING

Most security departments that require their staff to carry firearms only allow for and train for the use of pistols or less frequently, revolvers. Should your organization employ shotguns or rifles, then the training considerations become more complicated.

When looking for a firearms training metric and curriculum, the primary research should be your local jurisdiction and its regulations. Yes, your organization may supersede the requirements of a local jurisdiction but consider the benefits of ensuring the training you provide complies with your organization's higher authority and local regulations. Your training can and probably should surpass the regulatory training standards. Setting your standards to fit the organizational culture and environment is critical to effective training. Another consideration should be the age and physical capabilities of the staff. Many armed security positions are posted by retired law enforcement who may have movement limitations. So, equipment, weapons manipulation, and tactics may need to be modified for these issues.

Also, consider that the standard marksmanship training requirements of a state or municipality are generally static shooting at a paper target. Though this may be the elementary marksmanship skills training, it lacks the realistic need for a security officer to carry and use a firearm in the line of duty. Discussing cover and concealment is only a start to the tactics that should be taught to security personnel so that should they be involved in a gun battle their survival is increased.

A notable and standard firearm training curriculum can be found at the National Rifle Association (NRA). The curriculum offered by the NRA completely uses weapons terminology, safe handling, and shooting guidelines that are industry standards. Additionally, they offer shotgun and rifle courseware. However, the courses may only fulfill a part of the legal requirements for armed personnel in your state. And membership in the NRA may be a requirement to take the NRA courses.

The NRA also offers certificate training for Range Masters, Range Safety Officers (RSOs), and firearms instructors. A valuable aspect of the NRA courses is that they offer certification for those completing the course. These accreditations have been found to have value in the security profession as industry-recognized training curricula, testing, and certifications.

For firearms basics, the United States Concealed Carry Association (USCCA) also provides handgun training videos that cover terminology, definitions, safe handling, and guidelines. USCCA may also require membership to access their courseware. And again, it may fall short of the requirements of the states where your personnel are assigned.

Carrying a firearm for employment and the potential use of that weapon is probably the most litigious aspect of security. The training your organization provides, the curriculum you follow, the policies and procedures that the curriculum is based upon, the certification of the instructors, and the performance of the instruction staff are the strongest foundation for your department's armed contingencies. With the training, the training records become critical as proof that the training occurred, what topics were covered, who was in attendance, and their qualifications. Planning for these records to become critical evidence in court will hopefully provide mitigating factors to the legal defense of your company's actions and those of your staff members.

A course curriculum covering nomenclature, operational character-istics, safe handling, use of the weapon, loading and unloading, clearing of jams, the legal aspects of its possession, use within your organization, as well as marksmanship is a must. Just as with other courses you plan on providing, these also require documentation.

Should your organization decide to outsource this training, ensuring the purchased course will cover objectives required by your organization as well as the legal requirements of your state is your responsibility. Regardless of the contractor, your curriculum should still be developed and include the outsourced training documentation.

NOTE:
The use of a firearm is intended to stop violence by harming the aggressor. There is the potential for your staff and the aggressor to require lifesaving medical care. Combining a course on first aid is not only justified but potentially required by your organization and the jurisdiction in which your employees perform their service.

Define the Need

What risks are present that require your staff to carry firearms? An important question that requires a detailed answer in the form of a risk assessment and security survey. Recognizing that the legal basis for the use of deadly force is that it may only be used to protect the security staff carrying the weapon, or others from imminent danger of death or serious physical injury. Where in your organization does this potential threat exist and what other mitigating facts can be employed to reduce that possibility? If this fits your organization's environment, then start with a policy that dictates when force may be used.

A strongly worded Use of Force Policy for your organization should be vetted by the risk and legal departments. This is one policy that should not be borrowed from another organization. There are too many news articles, television shows, and movies that may influence your staff in determining what is considered a valid use of force. Unfortunately, too many movies and television shows improperly demonstrate the use of deadly force, therefore consider your curriculum needs to show why these entertain-ment episodes are wrong. The employees of your organization do not have the privilege of making up their reasons, your policy needs to be gospel. One example could be the issue of "stand your ground."

Though this may be a law in some states, is it one that your organization considers justifiable in all cases? Take away the ambiguity with a solid Use of Force Policy.

Conduct a Task Analysis

Start your research with the requirements of the state in which your employees will be armed. List those requirements as tasks. Add to the list the administrative handling of the weapons while on site such as storage, loading and unloading, holstering, use of the safety, discharge barrels, gun lockers for detention facilities, wearing the weapon when offsite for the business of your organization, and even what to do when using the restroom.

Determine the Training Form

A common firearms course starts with a lecture in a classroom setting, then moves to practical exercises, marksmanship basics, and finally qualifications at a range. Somewhere within the lecture period should be the specifics of your organization and the Use of Force Policy.

Firearms classes generally will discuss the use of force continuum. Review and seek approval that it is consistent with the force continuum in the Use of Force Policy that your organization has approved. Also, consider that the use of force continuum is not easily taught from the podium. Consider plenty of time for questions, answers, and discussion.

When budgeting, the cost of this training will include:

- Range Personnel – an average is one Range Master and one RSO per four active shooters. If training a dozen officers but only four are actively on the firing line, then only one RSO is needed, and the Range Master can also act as the RSO.
- The Range Rental – most public ranges may not want an instructional event during open range times. Special times or agreements to rent a portion of the range away from their daily commerce should be discussed in advance.
- Range Equipment – targets (two per shooter), ammunition to practice marksmanship skills and qualify, personal protection equipment (eye and hearing protection).
- Training Time – the employees attending the training are not at work therefore shift coverage will be required.

Weapons

The weapons to be carried by your employees while at work should be discussed. Will you allow your staff to provide their own personal weapons and holsters, or will your organization provide these? There are valid reasons for either scenario as well as consideration of both.

Weapons owned by the employee:

- Provide cost savings to your organization and it would be reasonable to assume the weapons owned by the employees are favorable to their ability to handle and shoot with accuracy.
- The cost savings continue by the employee providing a holster and duty belt for the weapon. This may also ensure comfort and wearability. However, do not assume that the holster is made to fit the weapon and is in good shape and with retention quality. If allowing personnel to provide their own weapon, a standard will be difficult to maintain.
- The weapon may have been customized to the owner's grip, trigger pull, sighting, and other characteristics to enhance the accuracy of the shooter and weapon. Some customizations can make a firearm unsafe for use in security. Reviewing the weapons for these issues should be a policy if employee-owned weapons are allowed.

Weapons and duty gear provided by your organization

- Allows for standardization and use by any employee or any shift.
- Allows for standardization of ammunition, duty belt, holster, and magazines or speed loaders.
- Will be properly maintained by your organization and customization kept to a minimum.

Develop Training Objectives

By now you probably have a good feel for why the training is necessary, the policies and procedures required for documentation, the training scenarios, the time to conduct the training, and all legal issues. Using the input from the task analysis, develop a cogent set of objectives for the training event. A terminal objective covering the whole program and then enabling objectives should be drafted to cover your organizational requirements, nomenclature, operation, safe handling, marksmanship, shooting stance, shooting grip, sighting, and trigger pull. Then a separate set of objectives should be created for practice drawing from the holster, re-holstering, loading, reloading, unloading, and shooting at the range.

NOTE:
Some retention holsters, due to the mechanism in the holster that allows for maximum retention from another person drawing the weapon while worn on the body, may require hours of practice to draw and re-holster.

Depending on your organization's physical environment, tactical application of movement through buildings, getting in and out of patrol vehicles, moving as a team, and reacting to active shooters or hostile visitors may be included in the initial or follow-on courses.

Write the Curriculum

After reviewing the task analysis, group the tasks into acceptable sections, or in this case lecture and practical. Itemize the tasks in an order that gives a commonsense flow to the information being imparted where one seemingly may come before the other or in a series on which they build on each other. Now, draft a listing of items to be covered in this training.

If an outside course is purchased or used for this training, place it as an addendum to the curriculum as a whole with the original letterhead or logo printed on the material to verify that nothing was changed by your organization that might reduce the value of that training. Items added to the course or defined by your organization should be documented in your syllabus.

Document the training for each task in your organization's formal training documentation while referring to the purchased curriculum.

Develop Testing

For firearms training, the main intent is that the whole team does the same tasks, in the same way allowing for no ambiguity which could create insecurity within your program. Testing in this subject would require a written test of the lecture portion and then an evaluation of the students' use of practical training and finally qualification on the range. Though not typically recorded in the qualification, observable poor safety handling should be noted and if performed improperly after correction could be considered a failure of the course.

Recertification

Skills such as using firearms are considered perishable if not practiced and may require a mandatory recertification from the municipality in which your organization is functioning. A recertification program should be included in the training curriculum. Using the experience of your peers and local law enforcement can give you an idea as to how frequently the retraining needs to be conducted. As an example, most law enforcement agencies require quarterly marksmanship training and qualification.

ELECTROSHOCK OR CONDUCTED ENERGY WEAPONS

Should your staff carry any weapons, such as a firearm, then also carrying an electroshock weapon can give the staff member a choice in which weapon is best suited for the situation and will cause the least injury to the aggressor. If your organization chooses to have staff carry electroshock weapons such as stun guns, or the TASER® line of weapons, then certification, training, and policies are required before carrying or using the weapon. Though considered non-lethal, or less-than-lethal weapons, the potential of injury requires specialized training initial certification, and periodic recertification.

Electroshock Weapons, commonly called "stun guns" are categorized as short handheld weapons with probes that when contacting a body and the trigger depressed will cause an electric shock to the person it touches. There are numerous variations of this, including rings, handheld devices, flashlights, cattle prods, batons, shotgun rounds, and weapons in the shape of a pistol that deploy (shoot) projectiles with wires connected to the weapon allowing an electric shock to be transmitted when the trigger is depressed.

Electroshock belts are commonly used in correctional facilities and when a subject is in transit. This is not a common security weapon.

For this section, we should consider stun guns as handheld weapons that administer electroshock when pressed against the subject's person and a trigger depressed or activated. The electroshock provided by the stun gun is painful and compliance is reached by the aggressor not wanting to be hurt. The performance of the weapon depends on the aggressor's pain threshold and state of mind as the pain is only felt when the weapon is used and is momentary.

TAZER® is an electroshock weapon that propels small dart-like projectiles so that when both strike a body the circuit is complete and produces an electric shock. The electroshock produced by the TAZER® causes paralysis or loss of muscle control causing the body to fall to the ground. The shock is momentary but has a short-lasting effect allowing time to gain compliance such as handcuffing.

Similar to carrying a firearm for employment, carrying an electroshock weapon, and the potential use of that weapon have a considerable litigious aspect on security. The training your organization provides, the curriculum you follow, the policies and procedures that the curriculum is based upon, the certification of the instructors, and the performance of the instruction staff are the strongest foundation for your department's policies, procedures, and daily practices. With the training, the training records become critical as proof that the training occurred, what topics were covered, who was in attendance, the certification of the instructor, and the attendee's qualifications. During legal proceedings, these records can become critical evidence in court and hopefully will provide mitigating findings.

A course curriculum covering nomenclature, operational characteristics, safe handling, testing, use of the weapon, after the weapon is used, and the legal aspects of its possession and use within your organization is a must. Just like other courses you are planning on providing, these also require documentation.

Should your organization decide to outsource this training, ensure the course covers objectives required by your organization as well as the legal requirements of your state. Regardless of the contractor, your curriculum should still be developed and include their documentation.

NOTE:
The use of an electroshock weapon is intended to stop violence by harming the aggressor. Though considered and sold as less-than-lethal or non-lethal weapons, there is the potential for your staff and the aggressor to require lifesaving medical care. Combining a course on first aid is not only justified but potentially required by your organization and the jurisdiction in which your employees perform their service.

It is not uncommon to find that an employee decides to carry an unauthorized weapon for self-defense. This should not be allowed unless you verify the training, and the electroshock weapon is of good quality and the output fits your organization's standards.

Define the Need

What risks are present that require your staff to carry an electroshock weapon? An important question that requires a detailed answer in the form of a risk assessment and security survey. Recognizing that the force delivered by these devices may only be used to protect yourself or others from the danger of death or serious physical injury and to necessitate compliance in effecting a lawful arrest. Where in your organization does this potential threat exist and what other mitigating facts can be employed to reduce that possibility? If this fits your organization's environment, then start with a policy that dictates when such force may be used.

A strongly worded Use of Force Policy for your organization should be vetted by the risk and legal departments. This is one policy that should be organic in its development and not be borrowed from another organization. There are too many news articles, television shows, and movies that may influence your staff in determining what is considered a valid use of force. Several entertainment shows demonstrate such a weapon being used solely for the purpose of inflicting pain. The employees of your organization do not have the privilege of making up their reasons, your policy needs to be gospel. If the weapon is used to bring an aggressor into compliance so that your staff can effect an arrest, how much compliance does your organization consider justifiable in all cases? Further use of the weapon without justification to induce pain can result in your employee being arrested for battery or assault. Take away the ambiguity with a solid Use of Force Policy.

Conduct a Task Analysis

Start your research with the requirements of the state in which your employees will be armed. List those requirements as tasks. Add to the list the administrative handling of the weapons while on site such as storage, testing, loading, and unloading, holstering, use of the safety, weapons lockers for detention facilities, wearing the weapon when offsite for the business of your organization, and even what to do when using the restroom.

Determine the Training Form

A common weapons course starts with a lecture in a classroom setting, then moves to practical exercises, and finally qualifications. Highlighted within the lecture period should be the specifics of your organization and discussion in the Use of Force Policy.

Weapons classes generally will discuss the use of force continuum. If using a contractor or product manufacturer's courseware, review and approve that the force continuum discussed in their curriculum is consistent with the force continuum in the Use of Force Policy that your organization has approved.

When budgeting the cost of this training will include:

- Certified Instructor.
- Training Room – most electroshock weapon training can be performed in a classroom setting. However, if the weapon projects darts, room for a target and standoff distance is required.
- Range Equipment – electroshock weapons that project darts require a target that is mounted on a surface. Classroom walls are not suited for this as the darts may injure the wall covering. Verify the number of training cartridges or magazines required per student. Consider personal protection equipment (eye protection).
- Training Time – the employees attending the training are not at work therefore shift coverage will be required.

Weapons

The electroshock weapon to be carried by your employees while at work should be discussed to determine the type and style. Should you allow your staff to provide their own electroshock weapon and holster or will your organization provide these? There are valid reasons for either scenario as well as consideration of both.

Electroshock Weapons owned by the employee:

- Provide cost savings to your organization and it would be reasonable to assume the weapons owned by the employees are favorable to their ability to handle and use with accuracy.
- Could also include the employee providing a holster and duty belt for the weapon. This may also ensure comfort and wear-ability. However, do not assume that the holster is made to fit the

weapon and is in good shape and with retention quality. If allowing personnel to provide their own weapon, a standard will be difficult to maintain

- The weapon may have been customized to the owner's grip, trigger pull, and other characteristics to enhance the accuracy of the shooter and weapon. Some customizations can make an electroshock weapon unsafe for use in security.
- Some electroshock weapons available on the market are not suitable for security use, such as cattle prods or low-price and low-quality manufacturing. Reviewing the weapons for these issues should be a policy if employee-owned weapons are allowed.

Weapons provided by your organization:

- Allows for standardization and use by any employee or any shift.
- Allows for standardization of cartridge, power output, battery charging, duty belt, and holster.
- It is common to find such weapons are a bright color, which identifies to witnesses, the aggressor, and security personnel that what the officer is deploying is not a firearm.
- Several new models come with multiple uses within the weapon. When first offered for use as a less-than-lethal weapon to security and law enforcement, the weapons only held one cartridge which after deployment had to be replaced. The newer models have two or three cartridges within the weapon allowing for use against multiple aggressors without reloading.
- Will be properly maintained by your organization and customization kept at a minimum.

Develop Training Objectives

Recognize the need for training through your research to develop the task analysis and the policies and procedures necessary for documentation, the training scenarios, the time to conduct the training, and all legal issues. Using the input from the task analysis, develop a cogent set of objectives for the training event. A terminal objective for the whole program and then enabling objectives should be drafted to cover your organizational requirements, then nomenclature, operation, safe handling, placement of the holster, shooting stance, grip, sighting, and trigger pull. Then a separate set of objectives should be created for practice from drawing the holster, re-holstering, testing, reloading, unloading, and practice firing the weapon.

NOTE:
Organizations where security staff carry a TAZER® and firearm, maintain that the TAZER® be carried on a cross-draw holster so that the officer does not draw the wrong weapon in haste.

Depending on your organization's physical environment, tactical application of movement through buildings, getting in and out of patrol vehicles, moving as a team, and effecting an arrest after which the weapon was discharged to necessitate compliance, removal of the projectile darts, and first aid for injuries sustained during the unintended consequences of the body's reaction to the electroshock may be included in follow-on courses.

Write the Curriculum

After a review of the task analysis, group the tasks into acceptable sections, or in this case lecture and practical. Itemize the tasks in an order that gives a commonsense flow to the information being imparted where one seemingly may come before the other or in a series on which they build on each other. Now, draft a listing of items to be covered in this training.

If an outside course is purchased or used for this training, place it as an addendum to the curriculum as a whole with the original letterhead or logo printed on the material to verify that nothing was changed by your organization that might reduce the value of that training. Items added to the course or defined by your organization should be documented in your syllabus.

Document the training for each task in your organization's formal training documentation.

Determine and Develop Testing

For electroshock weapons training, the main intent is that the whole team reacts similarly and takes the same steps to mitigate the event allowing for no ambiguity which could create insecurity within your program. Testing in this subject would require a written test of the lecture portion and then qualification with the weapon. Though not typically recorded in the qualification, observable poor safe handling should be noted and if performed improperly after correction could be considered a failure of the course.

Recertification

Skills such as using electroshock weapons may be perishable if not practiced and may require a mandatory recertification from the municipality in which your organization is functioning or the product manufacturer. A recertification program should be included in the training curriculum. Using the experience of your peers and local law enforcement can give you an idea as to how frequently the retraining needs to be conducted.

BATON AND IMPACT WEAPONS

Should your staff carry any weapons, such as a firearm, or electroshock weapon, the addition of an approved impact weapon, can give the staff member a choice in which weapon is best suited for the situation and will cause the least injury to the aggressor. If your organization chooses to have staff carry impact weapons commonly identified as a straight baton, handle baton, or the collapsible versions of either baton, then certification, training, and policies are required before carrying or using the weapon. Though considered non-lethal or less-than-lethal weapons, the potential of injury requires specialized training, practice with initial certification, and periodic recertification.

Impact weapons have fallen out of favor after high-profile cases of impact weapons being used on aggressors in the view of public television reporting and causing it to have shocking effects and the perception that it is used for punitive measures instead of the intended compliance and control over an aggressive person.

The straight baton, generally about 24" long, made of metal, wood, or plastic has been relatively replaced by the collapsible form of the baton. The collapsible baton can be made of metal and it is only about 10" long. Different models collapse using several sections of tubing, two to three sections made of metal are common. This allows for the weapon to be carried comfortably on the duty belt, and it takes the public stigma away from seeing security carrying what is seen as a club. To collapse the baton, some models have a button to allow it to collapse with minimal force. Others require the striking end to be forced against a solid object such as the pavement.

The handle baton has its origins as a martial arts weapon called a tonfa. The tonfa originated from a farm implement used to turn a grist mill, or a flail used to separate chaff from seed. In current martial arts training and competitions, tonfas are used in pairs.

Handle batons can be purchased either fixed with a 24″ length constructed of metal or plastic with a core to stiffen the weapon. The retractable version is also approximately 24″ but only retracts to about 13″. Some models require the depression of a button to collapse the baton others collapse with the striking end being pushed into a solid object like pavement.

Some states have specific training and certification requirements of approximately eight hours and include the use of the weapon, identifying the striking points on the body, where not to strike the body, first aid, laws regarding its use, and certification. Your company may want to follow the strictest standard your research uncovers as those standards may be identified in trial proceedings should the use of such a weapon result in legal action. When a due diligence search by the plaintiff reveals that your training is not as long or has fewer training topics your legal council will need to prove that the training your employee received is still just as comprehensive.

Similar to carrying a firearm or an electroshock weapon for employment, the potential use of an impact weapon has a considerable litigious aspect on security. The training your organization provides, the curriculum you follow, the policies and procedures that the curriculum is based upon, the certification of the instructors, and the performance of the instruction staff are the strongest foundation for your department's policies, procedures, and daily practices. With the training, the training records become critical as proof that the training occurred, what topics were covered, who was in attendance, the certification of the instructor, and the attendee's qualifications. During legal proceedings, these records can become critical evidence in court and hopefully will provide mitigating findings.

A course curriculum covering awareness of the weapon and how it may be viewed by the public, nomenclature, characteristics, safe handling, and retention, blocking and striking fundamentals, and the legal aspects of its possession and use within your organization is a must. With striking weapons, the portions of the body that should not intentionally be struck are a critical topic. Just like other courses you plan on providing, these also require documentation of the training.

One noted benefit of selecting an impact weapon over firearms is the age restriction of the user. Most states, if not all, require security to be 21 years of age to carry a firearm on duty; however, to be certified in a baton, 18 is the minimum age requirement in some states. Should your organization look at this issue favorably, a risk assessment must be completed to determine the true need to carry a striking weapon. If the assessment determines that a firearm is necessary for security to carry, then hiring someone under 21 who can only carry a striking weapon is an unnecessary risk to the employee and your organization.

Should your organization decide to outsource this training, ensure the course covers objectives required by your organization as well as the legal requirements of your state. Regardless of the contractor, your curriculum should still be developed and include their documentation.

NOTE:
The use of an impact weapon is intended to stop violence by harming the aggressor and effect control of a subject by using pain compliance with the assistance of the weapon. Though considered and sold as less-than-lethal or non-lethal weapons, there is the potential for your staff and the aggressor to require lifesaving medical care. Combining a course on first aid is not only justified but potentially required by your organization and the jurisdiction in which your employees perform their service.

It is not uncommon to find that an employee decides to carry an unauthorized impact weapon for self-defense. These can include saps, defensive pens, and kubaton (a palm-width fighting stick) sometimes with a pointed end or able to be used as a key ring. Research the use of and whether your organization will accept the risk of employees carrying such items. Saps or other small trudgens should not be allowed unless the state in which your organization resides allows such an item to be used by security. If this is the case, then your department should consider a training course that covers their use.

Define the Need

What risks are present that require your staff to carry an impact weapon? An important question that requires a detailed answer in the form of a risk assessment and security survey. Recognizing that the force delivered by such a weapon may only be used to protect the officer with the weapon or others from the danger of death or serious physical injury and to necessitate compliance in effecting a lawful arrest. Where in your organization does this potential threat exist and what other mitigating facts can be employed to reduce that possibility? If this fits your organization's environment, then start with a policy that dictates when such force may be used.

A strongly worded Use of Force Policy for your organization should be vetted by the risk and legal departments. This is one policy that should be organic in its development and not be borrowed from another organization. There are too many news articles, television shows, and movies that may influence your staff in determining what is considered a valid use of force. Unfortunately, too many entertainment shows demonstrate poor use of such weapons or their improper use to inflict unlawful pain. The employees of your organization do not have the privilege of making up their reasons, your policy needs to be gospel. If the weapon is used to bring an aggressor into compliance so that your staff can effect an arrest, how much compliance does your organization consider justifiable in all cases? Further use of the weapon without justification to induce pain can result in your employee being arrested for battery or assault. Take away the ambiguity with a solid Use of Force Policy.

Conduct a Task Analysis

Start your research with the requirements of the state in which your employees will be armed. List those requirements as tasks. Add to the list the administrative handling of the weapons while on site such as storage, holstering, weapons lockers for detention facilities, wearing the weapon when offsite for the business of your organization, and even what to do when using the restroom.

Determine the Training Form

A common weapons course starts with a lecture in a classroom setting, then moves to practical exercises, and finally qualifications. Highlighted within the lecture period should be the specifics of your organization and the Use of Force Policy.

Weapons classes generally will discuss the use of force continuum. If using a contractor or product manufacturer's courseware, review and approve that the force continuum discussed in their curriculum is consistent with the force continuum in the Use of Force Policy that your organization has approved.

When budgeting the cost of this training will include:

- Certified Instructor.
- Training Room – most impact weapon training can be performed in a classroom setting. However, the practice of the weapon carry, use and defensive blocks, compliance holds and acceptable striking points will require space ample for the class size.
- Range Equipment – impact weapons are generally not used to practice strikes due to the amount of injury to other equipment and personnel. Training batons, strike pads, and even body suits may need to be purchased for the training and recertification.
- Training Time – the employees attending the training are not at work therefore shift coverage will be required.

Weapons

The impact weapon to be carried by your employees while at work should be discussed to determine the type and style. Should you allow your staff to provide their own impact weapon and holster or will your organization provide these? There are valid reasons for either scenario as well as consideration of both.

Impact Weapons owned by the employee:

- Provide cost savings to your organization and it would be reasonable to assume the weapons owned by the employees are favorable to their ability to handle and use with accuracy.
- If the employee has their own baton, it may include a holster and duty belt for the weapon. This may also ensure comfort and wearability. However, do not assume that the holster is made to fit the weapon and is in good shape and with retention quality. If allowing personnel to provide their own weapon, a standard will be difficult to maintain.
- The weapon may have been customized to the owner's grip, striking point enhancements, and other characteristics to enhance the weapon's effectiveness. Some customizations can make an impact weapon unsafe for use in security. Some impact weapons available on the market are not suitable for security use, such as low-price and low-quality manufacturing. Reviewing the weapons for these issues should be a policy if employee-owned weapons are allowed.

Weapons provided by your organization:

- Allows for standardization and use by any employee or any shift.
- Allows for standardization of duty belts and holsters.
- Properly maintained by your organization and customization kept at a minimum.

Develop Training Objectives

Recognize the need for training through your research to develop the task analysis and the policies and procedures necessary for documentation, the training scenarios, the time to conduct the training, and all legal issues. Using the input from the task analysis, develop a cogent set of objectives for the training event. A terminal objective for the whole program and then enabling objectives should be drafted to cover your organizational requirements, then nomenclature, safe handling, weapons retention, placement of the holster, stance, grip, swing, and striking points. Then a separate set of objectives should be created for practice drawing the holster, re-holstering, and practicing with the weapon.

Depending on your organization's physical environment, tactical application of movement through buildings, getting in and out of patrol vehicles, moving as a team, and effecting an arrest after which the weapon was used to necessitate compliance, first aid for injuries sustained during the use of the impact weapon may be included in the course or in follow-on courses.

Write the Curriculum

After reviewing the task analysis, group the tasks into acceptable sections, or in this case lecture and practical exercise. Itemize the tasks in an order that gives a commonsense flow to the information being imparted where one seemingly may come before the other or in a series on which they build on each other. Now, draft a listing of items to be covered in this training.

If an outside course is purchased or used for this training, place it as an addendum to the curriculum as a whole with the original letterhead or logo printed on the material to verify that nothing was changed by your organization that might reduce the value of that training. Items added to the course or defined by your organization should be documented in your syllabus.

Document the training for each task in your organization's formal training documentation.

Determine and Develop Testing

For impact weapons training, the main intent is that the whole team reacts similarly and takes the same steps to mitigate the event allowing for no ambiguity which could create a risk or insecurity within your program. Testing in this subject would require a written test of the lecture portion and then qualification with the weapon. Though not typically recorded in the qualification, observable poor safe handling, and inappropriate statements made during the practice should be noted, and if repeated or performed improperly after correction could be considered a failure of the course.

Recertification

Skills such as using impact weapons may be perishable if not practiced and may require mandatory recertification from the municipality in which your organization is functioning. A recertification program should be included in the training curriculum. Using the experience of your peers and local law enforcement can give you an idea as to how frequently the retraining needs to be conducted.

CHEMICAL SPRAYS/TEAR GAS/OLEORESIN SPRAY

Should your staff carry any weapons, such as a firearm, electroshock weapon, or impact weapon, the addition of an approved chemical spray can give the staff member a choice in which weapon is best suited for the situation and will cause the least injury to the aggressor. Whether carried by itself or in conjunction with another weapon, the training required for the carrying of a chemical spray will include certification, training, and policies before carrying or using the weapon. Though considered non-lethal, or less-than-lethal weapons, the potential of injury requires specialized training, and decontamination actions with practice during the initial certification, and then periodic recertification.

The most common chemical spray weapon available for security is OC spray, normally called "pepper spray" as capsicum is the herb that produces chili and bell peppers to be spicy. The percentage of OC and capsaicin components to the propellant, the effective standoff distance of the stream to the target, whether the canister deploys a spray or stream, is the propellent oil or water-based, and even the Scoville Heat Units (SHU) may be qualities to consider when selecting the weapon.

Additional chemical weapons that may still be in production include:

- CS Gas – The compound 2-chlorobenzalmalononitrile, a cyano-carbon, is the defining component of tear gas commonly referred to as CS gas, which is used as a riot control agent.
- CN Gas – Phenacyl chloride, also commonly known as chlor-oacetophenone, is a substituted acetophenone. It is a useful building block in organic chemistry. Apart from that, it has been historically used as a riot control agent, where it is designated CN. It should not be confused with cyanide, another agent used in chemical warfare, which has the chemical structure of CN.
- Mace® – The CN Gas compound in a percentage to allow for effective personal protection in most environments. It was developed in 1960.

OC spray canisters come in a variety of sizes. Common for carrying on a duty belt is the 3-ounce size with a twist cap or other form of safety from inadvertent deployment.

Some states have specific training and certification requirements amounting to approximately two hours that include the use of the weapon, aiming points on the body, first aid with decontamination procedures, laws about its use, and certification requirements.

Similar to carrying any weapon, the potential use of a chemical agent has some negative litigious aspects on security, such as its use in an enclosed environment and affecting non-aggressive personnel in the space. The training your organization provides, the curriculum you follow, the policies and procedures that the curriculum is based upon, the certification of the instructors, and the performance of the instruction staff are the strongest foundation for your department's policies, proce-dures, and daily practices. With the training, the training records become critical as proof that the training occurred, what topics were covered, who was in attendance, the certification of the instructor, and the attendee's qualifications. During legal proceedings, these records can become critical evidence in court and hopefully will provide mitigating findings.

A course curriculum covering awareness of the weapon, nomenclature, characteristics, safe handling and retention, fundamentals, first aid/decontamination, and the legal aspects of its possession and use within your organization is a must. Just like other courses you are planning on providing, these also require documentation.

One noted benefit of selecting a chemical spray weapon over firearms is the age restriction of the user and the general availability for the public to purchase and carry the weapon. Most states, if not all, require security to be 21 years of age to carry a firearm on duty; however, to be certified in chemical spray weapons, 18 is the minimum age requirement in some states. Should your organization look at this issue favorably, a risk assessment must be completed to determine the true need to carry any weapon. If the assessment determines that a firearm is necessary, then hiring someone under 21 who can only carry a chemical spray weapon is an unnecessary risk to the employee and your organization.

Should your organization decide to outsource this training, ensure the course covers objectives required by your organization as well as the legal requirements of your state. Regardless of the contractor, your curriculum should still be developed and include their documentation.

NOTE:
The use of a chemical spray weapon is intended to stop violence by harming the aggressor and effect control of a subject by using pain compliance with the assistance of the weapon. Though considered and sold as less-than-lethal or non-lethal weapons, there is the potential for your staff and the aggressor to require lifesaving medical care and decontamination. Combining a course on first aid and decontamination is not only justified but potentially required by your organization and the jurisdiction in which your employees perform their service.

There is always a chance that the security staff member when deploying any chemical spray toward an aggressive subject may find that the wind direction was not favorable for the chemical spray deployment and that your personnel are hit by and affected by the chemical. Learning to fight or operate through the effects of the spray should be considered.

It is not uncommon to find that an employee decides to carry an unauthorized chemical spray weapon for self-defense. These can include keychain canisters, pen canisters, and even large bear spray canisters. These should not be allowed unless your organization verifies the training and accepts that your employees' use of such additional weapons fits your organization's standards.

Define the Need

What risks are present that require your staff to carry a chemical spray weapon? An important question that requires a detailed answer in the form of a risk assessment and security survey. Recognizing that the force delivered by such a weapon may only be used to protect your officer or others from the danger of death or serious physical injury and to necessitate compliance in effecting a lawful arrest. Where in your organization does this potential threat exist and what other mitigating facts can be employed to reduce that possibility? If this fits your organization's environment, then start with a policy that dictates when such force may be used.

A strongly worded Use of Force Policy for your organization should be vetted by the risk and legal departments. This is one policy that should be organic in its development and not be borrowed from another organization. There are too many news articles, television shows, and movies that may influence your staff in determining what is considered a valid use of force. The employees of your organization do not have the privilege of making up their reasons or mimicking what they have seen during a show produced for entertainment, your policy needs to be gospel. If the weapon is used to bring an aggressor into compliance so that your staff can effect an arrest, how much compliance does your organization consider justifiable in all cases? Further use of the weapon without justification to induce pain can result in your employee being arrested for battery or assault. Take away the ambiguity with a solid Use of Force Policy.

Conduct a Task Analysis

Start your research with the requirements of the state in which your employees will be armed. List those requirements as tasks. Add to the list the administrative handling of the weapons while on site such as storage, holstering, weapons lockers for detention facilities, wearing the weapon when offsite for the business of your organization, and even what to do when using the restroom.

Determine the Training Form

A common weapons course starts with a lecture in a classroom setting, then moves to practical exercises, and finally qualifications. Highlighted within the lecture period should be the specifics of your organization and the Use of Force Policy.

Weapons classes generally will discuss the use of force continuum. If using a contractor or product manufacturer's courseware, review and approve that the force continuum discussed in their curriculum is consistent with the force continuum in the Use of Force Policy that your organization has approved.

When budgeting, the cost of this training will include:

- Certified Instructor.
- Training Room – most chemical weapon training can be performed in a classroom setting. However, the practice of the weapons carry, use and acceptable aiming points will require space ample for the class size.
- Practical Application Equipment – so that the actual chemical spray weapons are not used for practice, training canisters are available that mirror the trigger safety, distance, and projected spray patterns for use in the classroom.

    Most law enforcement agencies in the United States require that during the academy, trainees feel the effects of the chemical spray weapon that they carry. Should your organization consider this training action, describe in the objectives the benefit of such action.
- Training Time – the employees attending the training are not at work therefore shift coverage will be required.

Weapons

The chemical spray weapon to be carried by your employees while at work should be discussed to determine the type and style. Should you allow your staff to provide their own chemical spray weapon and holster or will your organization provide these? There are valid reasons for either scenario as well as consideration of both.

Chemical Spray Weapons owned by the employee:

- Provides a small cost savings to your organization and it would be reasonable to assume the weapons owned by the employees are favorable to their ability to handle and use with accuracy.

- The employee could also provide a holster and duty belt for the weapon. This may also ensure comfort and wearability. However, do not assume that the holster is made to fit the weapon and is in good shape and with retention quality. If allowing personnel to provide their own weapon, a standard will be difficult to maintain.
- It is doubtful, but the weapon may have been customized to the owner's grip, and other characteristics to enhance the weapon's effectiveness. Any customization can make a chemical spray weapon unsafe for use in security. Some chemical spray weapons available on the market are not suitable for security use, such as low-price and low-quality manufacturing. Reviewing the weapons for these issues should be a policy if employee-owned weapons are allowed.

Weapons provided by your organization:

- Chemical spray weapons are affordable.
- Allows for standardization and use by any employee or any shift.
- Allows for standardization of duty belts and holsters.
- Will be properly maintained by your organization and customization kept at a minimum.
- Ensured that the correct chemical spray was being deployed based on the environment and other weapons. An example of this is if the officer is also carrying an electroshock weapon, then water-based chemical spray should be considered.

Develop Training Objectives

Recognize the need for training through your research to develop the task analysis and the policies and procedures necessary for documentation, the training scenarios, the time to conduct the training, and all legal issues. Using the input from the task analysis, develop a cogent set of objectives for the training event. A terminal objective for the whole program and then enabling objectives should be drafted to cover your organizational requirements, then nomenclature, operation, safe handling/retention, placement of the holster, stance, grip, and aiming points. Then a separate set of objectives should be created for practice drawing the holster, re-holstering, and practicing with the weapon, first aid, and decontamination steps.

Depending on your organization's physical environment, tactical application of movement through buildings, getting in and out of patrol vehicles, moving as a team, and effecting an arrest after which the weapon was used to necessitate compliance, and first aid for injuries sustained during the use of the chemical spray weapon and decontamination of the arrestee, and security personnel may be included in follow-on courses.

Write the Curriculum

After reviewing the task analysis, group the tasks into acceptable sections, or in this case lecture and practical. Itemize the tasks in an order that gives a commonsense flow to the information being imparted where one seemingly may come before the other or in a series on which they build on each other. Now, draft a listing of items to be covered in this training.

If an outside course is purchased or used for this training, place it as an addendum to the curriculum as a whole with the original letterhead or logo printed on the material to verify that nothing was changed by your organization that might reduce the value of that training. Items added to the course or defined by your organization should be documented in your syllabus.

Document the training for each task in your organization's formal training documentation.

Develop Testing

For chemical spray weapons training, the main intent is that the whole team reacts similarly and takes the same steps to mitigate the event allowing for no ambiguity which could create a risk or insecurity within your program. Testing in this subject would require a written test of the lecture portion and then qualification with the weapon.

Recertification

Skills such as using chemical sprays/tear gas/oleoresin spray may require a mandatory recertification from the municipality in which your organization is functioning. A recertification program should be included in the training curriculum. Using the experience of your peers and local law enforcement can give you an idea as to how frequently the retraining needs to be conducted.

FIRST AID, CPR, AND AED

As a service to your organization's employees and customers, security staff often hold first aid and CPR certifications which now often includes the use of an Automatic Electronic Deliberator (AED). According to the Red Cross and American Heart Association (AHA), your staff should recertify every two years. Since changes in medical practices and practical application of first aid, CPR, and an AED, the review of these skills will require recertification. A second reason for recertification is the advances in science in the methodology of CPR and the various types of AEDs in use. The old use of fifteen compressions and two breaths for one-person CPR and five compressions to one breath for two-person CPR has been changed and is likely to continue changing with medical updates. Keeping current with changes is critical to saving a life, reducing injury to the victim, and reducing personal and organizational liability.

The AED is, as the name implies, automatic. Accompanying directions with graphics has been deemed easy so that anyone can position the pads correctly, and the AED does all the rest. Additionally, the AED will remind the rescuer to call 9-1-1, where to place the two pads, and other critical steps that may be forgotten during the excitement of the rescue.

At one time the Red Cross and AHA were the only certifying bodies for these courses. That has changed and there are a variety of companies that are proven and will provide certification and recertification. When choosing a provider, observe a class being given and verify the instructor's method of teaching, completeness of the instruction, and oversight during the practical application. Hiring a company that guarantees a quick class may help your man-hours per class but it may not help your organization in a legal matter when testimony that the instructor did not require practice or the class was a study of how fast your staff can get their certification card.

Broken ribs and death are common after CPR is performed, even when performed correctly. AEDs are not always successful in resuscitating a victim as the AED only provides electroshock to bring the heart back into rhythm. If the heart is not in defibrillation, then the AED will be ineffective. Initiating CPR would be the next step to resuscitation as CPR will function as a beating heart circulating oxygenated blood. Knowing that there is a possibility that lifesaving methods may not be helpful, also brings the actions of your staff into a possible legal battle, though many states adhere to a "Good Samaritan" rule.

First aid courses provided to security staff are also common. Though many of your security staff may have received combat first aid training in the military, the class is still needed for certification and periodic recertification. With Emergency Medical Services just a phone call away, the initial assessment and protection of a wound and making an injured party comfortable has become the primary function of the first aid provider. Your organization's industry, function, and operational employment will dictate the necessity of a first aid recertification schedule.

Should your security employees carry weapons, attention to providing first aid after the weapon is used is necessary. Also, should your employees carry firearms, the use and carrying of a tourniquet should be considered.

A course curriculum covering first aid, CPR, and AED as well as other lifesaving measures for your organization is a must. Just as with other courses you plan on providing, these also require documentation. A general course objective should be incorporated into the curriculum from your provider.

Define the Need

What needs are present that require your staff to be certified in CPR, first aid, and the use of AED? A major implied role of security is to protect the employees and visitors to your organization. That protection includes knowing what to do when an emergency event occurs. In industrial operations, there may be an increased risk of injury. If this fits your organization's environment, then start with a policy that dictates a wide variety of instances that require medical assistance from security personnel. The policy may include a statement that the organization expects the security personnel to provide that medical assistance as dictated by the training they receive.

Conduct a Task Analysis

Research the requirements of the state in which your employees will be deployed to determine if such training is required. List any specific tasks your organization determines are in addition to the standard first aid, CPR, and AED training. These additional requirements may include dealing with injury from electricity, and the emergency shut-off locations of machinery and pumps. Add to the list the administrative handling of AEDs, trauma bags, and first aid kit inventories.

Determine the Training Form

First aid, CPR, and AED courses are generally lecture-based in a classroom setting, move to practical exercises, and finally qualifications. The use of video is also common as it grants greater continuity to the training and reduces by-passing minor but crucial points. Highlighted within the lecture period should be the specifics of your organization's policy.

When budgeting, the cost of this training will include:

- Certified Instructor.
- Training Room – most of the training is in a classroom setting with room for practical training with CPR mannequins, as necessary.
- Training Time – the employees attending the training are not at work therefore shift coverage will be required.

AED

The Automatic Electronic Defibrillator (AED) units may be determined by the building code and the industry in which your organization provides protection. The locations where such equipment and signage may be deployed can be covered by a municipal code, but generally, they should be in common spaces where they can be retrieved by anyone during an emergency. Connecting a magnetic contact so that an alarm is triggered to announce that an AED may be in use and its location is helpful for security to assist in a rescue.

AEDs have an expiration date. Calendaring these dates to ensure compliance, continued usefulness, and replacement is part of their maintenance schedule.

First Aid Kits/Trauma Bags

First aid kits in patrol vehicles and in some areas where organizational personnel have access may be required by municipal code. Commonly, employees will retrieve items from first aid kits for personal use, such as band-aids and aspirins. Ensuring the first aid kits are restocked for their continued use is important. If an emergency requires a drastic depletion of supplies, security should recognize the use and have it replaced as soon as possible.

Your organization may purchase and deploy trauma kits based on an as-needed basis. Trauma kits are generally fitted with consumables to protect wounds, tourniquets, airway tubes, and other devices that may require additional training to use and administer.

Develop Training Objectives

Recognize the need for training through your research developed during the task analysis and the policies and procedures required for documentation, the training scenarios, the time to conduct the training, and all legal issues. Using the input from the task analysis, develop a cogent set of objectives for the training event. A terminal objective for the whole program and then enabling objectives should be drafted to cover your organizational requirements, first aid, CPR, AED, and additional items such as first aid kits and trauma bags.

Depending on your organization's physical environment, tactical application of movement through buildings, getting in and out of patrol vehicles, moving as a team, and effecting an arrest after which a weapon was discharged to necessitate compliance, first aid requirements for injuries sustained from the event may be included in follow-on courses.

Write the Curriculum

After reviewing the task analysis, group the tasks into acceptable sections, or in this case lecture and practical. Itemize the tasks in an order that gives a commonsense flow to the information being imparted where one seemingly may come before the other or in a series on which they build on each other. Now, draft a listing of items to be covered in this training.

There is a strong chance that an outside course will be purchased or used for this training, place it as an addendum to the curriculum as a whole with the original letterhead or logo printed on the material to verify that nothing is changed by your organization that might reduce the value of that training. Items added to the course or defined by your organization should be documented in your syllabus.

Document the training for each task in your organization's formal training documentation.

Determine and Develop Testing

Testing for these subjects would require a written test of the lecture portion then skills performance and finally qualification.

Recertification

Skills such as first aid/CPR/AED have mandatory recertification. A recertification program should be included in the training curriculum. Use the experience of your instructors and contract company if you are employing an outside agency to perform the training.

HANDCUFFING/SELF-DEFENSE

Employees responsible for the security of your organization may come across a situation where they must defend themselves and place a person in handcuffs to affect an arrest. Should your employees carry handcuffs then there must be ample training in the correct use of the restraints. If the employee carries handcuffs, then self-defense course-work must also be provided as the percentage of arrestees that become violent during handcuffing is a considerable risk. When training your staff in handcuffing and self-defense there are a few items you should consider.

- If the employee is armed with any weapon (baton, OC spray, firearm, etc.) and you choose not to offer training in self-defense, then your employee may have no choice but to use their weapon instead of attempting to control a subject by using hand-to-hand methods or to defend themselves from attack. As a matter of risk avoidance, if your employee is carrying any weapon there should be a portion of the weapon training in self-defense, open-hand tactics, and de-escalation methods.
- Handcuffing a subject has specific requirements under the law. Those requirements need to be added to the curriculum and testing, such as the period of detention, mandatory notification of law enforcement, and what offering the arrested should be granted.
- Self-defense and handcuff training can cause injury to the employee or another with whom they are training. A licensed or certified instructor may mitigate injuries through slow move-ments and strict supervision. However, ensure your risk depart-ment is aware of the training.
- Self-defense and handcuff training will require a venue with ample room and padding to mitigate injuries.

145

- To minimize injuries to a self-defense or handcuff training partner, padded handheld striking pads and targets will be needed.
- To minimize injuries, prior to any self-defense and handcuff training, a period of stretching to get muscles and joints warmed up for the exercise.
- Due to the increased frequency of physical attacks, healthcare employees and airline employees are being provided with self-defense training. Should the post your employee is assigned be known as a hazardous location, providing self-defense should be considered.
- Self-defense and handcuff training should only be practiced under the watchful eye of a trainer. Allowing employees to practice outside of the training event and in the view of other employees, visitors, and management can cause supervisory problems.
- Handcuffing an unwilling person for practice may have criminal implications; therefore, practice should be conducted only with a knowledgeable training partner.
- At no time should a training partner be kept in handcuffs beyond the needs of training.
- A Use of Force Policy must be drafted, approved, and introduced during each self-defense training class. This may include the force continuum which dictates an escalation of force only when necessary, based on the aggressive behavior.
- A Use of Restraints Policy must be introduced and included in the training.
- Should your employees be required to defend themselves, the aggressor should be arrested, or a criminal complaint filed to cover the legalities of the event.
- A person defending themself from an aggressor can quickly become the aggressor and potentially be arrested for that action. Knowing the limits to which your organization considers self-defense is critically important. Improper use of handcuffs may be considered unlawful detention or even kidnapping. Ensuring that local laws are covered in the training is critical to ensure their legal use.
- When faced with a weapon, open-hand self-defense methods may have little value. Teaching this important fact may seem unnecessary; however, this point needs to be stated.

Define the Need

As in any training, the first step should be to draft a statement dictating the need to provide self-defense training. Determining the need will come from the interaction that has been documented within your organization. Contact local businesses, law enforcement agencies, and other security professionals as to incidents they have experienced and what they have identified for this need, incidents that they may have encountered and do they provide the training.

Conduct a Task Analysis

You may need extra research to determine what part of self-defense needs to be trained as well as what your risk and legal department will accept. Simply using a local martial arts studio may seem to solve the issue of training; however, they typically work on long-term practice and introduction of skills at a slower rate than your company may find acceptable.

When entertaining self-defense and handcuffing training programs from vendors or what other organizations may do in-house, consider if the training is sufficient or potentially too much for your organizational needs. Using the information, you receive from peers and law enforcement is a good method to determine what training is needed.

Training Format

To determine the form your training event will take there will need to be room for exercise, but remember to start by reviewing your policies for the use of force, use of handcuffs, any reporting that may be necessary, and arrest procedures. Taking the time to review these issues before training will put the reality of what happens when there is a laying on of hands or restraints. The time covering these topics may reduce the employee's willingness to use self-defense and place greater concentration and importance on de-escalating techniques.

Your training form could start with an hour of lecture with follow-up testing to ensure comprehension of the policies and procedures. The lab time is where the techniques of self-defense and handcuffing can be demonstrated and practiced.

Develop Training Objectives

A terminal objective describing why self-defense and handcuff training has been determined to be required for the position should be drafted with appropriate highlights for the course.

Enabling objectives should cover the portions of the course. Policy, hand and wrist locks, defensive actions, stance, disarming techniques, kicks, reaction times and distances, and de-escalation (not in this order) should be included. The handcuffing course will include stance, position of the arrestee, which handcuffs are permitted by your organization, double locking, and where a handcuffed person will be placed until law enforcement arrives.

Supervisors should be knowledgeable at a higher level when a handcuffed person is seated and under their protection until law enforcement can arrive. Also, this section should cover specifics as to the questioning of handcuffed subjects by management to discuss the handcuffing incident, when the handcuffs can be removed, and care for the restrained person.

NOTE:
Reminding your staff that there is no legal requirement to advise an arrestee of their rights under the Constitution may be critical, as doing so can cause legal issues for the forthcoming arresting law enforcement officer.

Write the Curriculum

Every step of the course should be documented in the curriculum. This will allow for consistency in the training and especially techniques. As there are several martial arts, having one instructor teach a method alien to the syllabus has complications when used in the field or an injury is incurred.

If a sub-contractor has been chosen to teach the course, make that training course syllabus part of your curriculum without changing or editing the documentation. Leaving text on their letterhead or logoed handouts is advisable. This does not mean that you cannot add it to your curriculum, just do not change anything as a risk mitigator.

Determine and Develop Testing

A written test covering policies should be included to ensure comprehension of your organization's allowable level of defense. The exercises and practice to master the defensive techniques should be completed to a satisfactory level. A level to which the instructor and management agree.

Handcuffing should be separately tested to ensure comprehension of the organization's policies, the ramifications of improper use of restraints, and technical expertise in their use and care.

Recertification

Skills such as self-defense and handcuffing are perishable if not practiced. A recertification program should be included in the training curriculum. Using the experience of your peers and local law enforcement can give you an idea as to how frequently the retraining needs to be conducted.

TACTICAL COMMUNICATION/DE-ESCALATION

The use of correct language and the choice of words during an exciting and stressful event can have an extremely calming effect on the situation. When I first started as a police officer, during a traffic stop you would immediately ask the driver for their driver's license and vehicle registration. This would immediately start a confrontational question "why did you stop me?" To which the common answer of the time was, "after you give me your license and registration, I will tell you." And sometimes, this could end up in a very aggressive exchange that took a simple traffic stop into something much more.

Then I was introduced to "Verbal Judo®." Verbal Judo and the Verbal Judo Institute started professing the use of language and word choice to reduce aggressive incidents. Verbal Judo introduced the use of tactical communications to reduce confrontation and increase cooperation.

It is not uncommon, that when a person comes into contact with police officers or security personnel, there may be fear or defensiveness as that the person does not want to be contacted or impeded or is told that they can or cannot do something. Astynomiaphobia is an established fear of law enforcement and in some people can cause panic resulting in increased heart rate, perspiration, trembling, choking sensation, tightness of the chest, nausea, hyperventilation, and a rise in blood pressure to name a few symptoms. That person, not understanding that they have this phobia, will revert to fight, or flight and their response will be defensive or aggressive.

With training in tactical communication, the traffic stop scenario was changed to a friendly hello, an introduction naming the department I worked for, and the reason for the stop. "Hello, I am Officer Bob of the Short Police Department, and the reason I stopped you was your brake lights are not working. May I see your driver's license and vehicle registration." Starting the conversation in a friendly tone reduces the fight or flight and may reduce a potential aggressive exchange.

Educating your staff and practicing tactical communications will increase the social benefit of your security department as security's role should be seen as more of a customer service-oriented role than policy enforcement. And when policy enforcement is an issue, tactical communication can reduce a defensive posture and increase the offender's cooperation.

De-escalation by using tactical communications is a means of managing all situations but is mostly pointed toward calming a person exhibiting the behavior of excitement, defense, or aggression. De-escalation tactics, when practiced, can effectively be used in all situations regardless of why the person's behavior is out of the norm. Training is beneficial to identify the objective symptoms of a person who was just a victim of a crime, a person who was just traumatized by an event, or those having a medical or psychological episode.

When interacting with a person exhibiting aggressive behavior, some consider the steps of validating their concern, fear, or needs, giving options for their actions, and then allowing the person to choose an option. Unfortunately, in law enforcement and policy enforcement, the options given to them may be narrowed by the law such as they cannot just walk away. When describing the options to the person, selling the options is also a communication tactic that can cover their limitations.

De-escalation training was recently mandated for U.S. Law enforcement. Specifically, the bill cited its use for "incidents that involve the unique needs of individuals who have a mental illness or cognitive deficit" (H.R. 5682 – 115th Congress (2017–2018) FIRST STEP Act).

De-escalation techniques also affect the security staffer who is using it on an individual, as it can calm their behavior, demeanor, voice, and body movements. All of which can be mirrored to calm the person to whom they are speaking. Removing the negative public view of security is the purpose of de-escalation tactics.

Define the Need

Why is this training necessary for your department personnel? In any training, the first step should be to draft a statement dictating the need to provide training for Tactical Communications/De-escalation Techniques. Determining the need will come from interactions that have been documented within your organization where an aggressive person identified that security personnel was part of the problem, or when an internal or external customer complains about the lack of helpfulness of security personnel during an incident. It may also be advantageous to contact industry peers, law enforcement agencies, and other security professionals as to the usefulness of such training and incidents that would have benefitted from trained staff in these topics.

Conduct a Task Analysis

The task analysis should determine what the training needs to include. This may require extra research to determine what part of tactical communications and de-escalation skills need to be included in the training as well as what your legal department will accept.

When entertaining tactical communication and de-escalation training programs from vendors or what other organizations may do in-house, consider if the training is sufficient or potentially too much for your organizational needs. Using the information you receive from peers and law enforcement is a good method to determine what training is needed. The vendor may also point out that with additional training the security staff can use their voice in de-escalating situations.

Develop Training Objectives

A terminal objective describing why de-escalation and tactical communication skills training was determined to be required for the position and the appropriate highlights of the course.

Enabling objectives should cover the portions of the course. Policy, empathy, active listening skills, tactical pause, awareness, understanding, and then reacting should be included. Additionally, it should cover the positive aspects of using open-ended instead of closed-ended questions. The course may also include taking an unassuming stance while still being safe, allowing the person to pace, sit, or lay down for comfort, and seeking medical attention or law enforcement assistance should that be necessary.

Supervisors should be knowledgeable at a higher level if law enforcement is needed.

Write the Curriculum

Every step of the course should be documented in the curriculum. This will allow for consistency in the training and especially practices and techniques. As there are tactical communication styles, having one instructor teach a method alien to the syllabus has complications when used in the field.

If a sub-contractor has been chosen to teach the course, make that training course syllabus a part of your curriculum without changing or editing the documentation. Leaving text on their letterhead or logoed handouts is advisable. This does not mean that you cannot add it to your curriculum, just do not change anything as a risk mitigator.

Develop Testing

A written test covering policies should be included to ensure comprehension of your organization's requirement to use tactical communication and de-escalation techniques. A policy on customer service may also be included in this course. The exercises and practice to master the techniques should be completed to a satisfactory level, a level to which the instructor and management agree.

Recertification

Skills such as these are perishable if not practiced and easily bypassed if security personnel are not well supervised. A recertification program should be included in the training curriculum and a section of the employee review might be tailored to address the employee's continued use of customer service and speaking to others. Using the experience of your peers and local law enforcement can give you an idea as to how frequently the retraining needs to be conducted.

9

Additional Training Alternatives/Additions

INTRODUCTION

You may have guessed that I am in favor of constant and consistent training. But we all know that you cannot keep teaching your staff the same topics over and over again, it is boring and at some point, they get nothing from being told the same things repetitively. So, how do you provide constant training while coming up with new topics, and minimize overtime or extra hours to cover the training time?

This section of the book will cover a constant training syllabus using a few tried and true training options. They include:

- Tactical Decision Games (TDGs)
- Required Reading

Add these to recurring training such as marksmanship, self-defense, handcuffing, baton training, CPR, first aid, and automatic electronic defibrillator (AED).

Putting together a schedule of these training courses into an annual calendar will give a complete picture of the training your department will receive during the year and will assist in formulating a budget for training your staff (Figure 9.1).

DOI: 10.4324/9781003292586-12

Annual Security Training Schedule

January	February	March
New Hires	New Hires	New Hires
Security Academy	Security Academy	Security Academy
FTO	FTO	FTO
Basic Marksmanship	Basic Marksmanship	Basic Marksmanship
Existing Staff	Existing Staff	Existing Staff
Advanced Marksmanship	Shotgun / Carbine	Firearms Qualification
CPO Study	CPO Study	CPO Study
All Security Staff	All Security Staff	All Security Staff
Required Reading	Required Reading	Required Reading
TDG Topic 1	TDG Topic 2	TDG Topic 3
Supervisors / Management	Supervisors / Management	Supervisors / Management
Required Reading	Required Reading	Required Reading
New Laws	HR Update	Advanced Fire System
CPP Study	CPP Study	CPP Study

April	May	June
New Hires	New Hires	New Hires
Security Academy	Security Academy	Security Academy
FTO	FTO	FTO
Basic Marksmanship	Basic Marksmanship	Basic Marksmanship
Existing Staff	Existing Staff	Existing Staff
Self Defense- Handcuffing	Patrol Procedures	Firearms Qualification
CPO Study	CPO Study	CPO Study
All Security Staff	All Security Staff	All Security Staff
Required Reading	Required Reading	Required Reading
TDG Topic 4	TDG Topic 5	TDG Topic 6
Supervisors / Management	Supervisors / Management	Supervisors / Management
Required Reading	Required Reading	Required Reading
Conducting Evaluations	Tactical Security Planning	Training Audit
CPP Study	CPP Study	CPP Study

Figure 9.1 Example annual security training schedule.

July	August	September
New Hires	*New Hires*	*New Hires*
Security Academy	*Security Academy*	*Security Academy*
FTO	*FTO*	*FTO*
Basic Marksmanship	*Basic Marksmanship*	*Basic Marksmanship*
Existing Staff	*Existing Staff*	*Existing Staff*
Advanced Marksmanship	*Shotgun / Carbine*	*Firearms Qualification*
CPO Study	*CPO Study*	*CPO Study*
All Security Staff	*All Security Staff*	*All Security Staff*
TASER Recert	*Required Reading*	*Required Reading*
TDG Topic 7	*TDG Topic 8*	*TDG Topic 9*
Supervisors / Management	*Supervisors / Management*	*Supervisors / Management*
Required Reading	*Required Reading*	*Required Reading*
Marketing	*Intelligence Briefing*	*Conducting Investigations*
CPP Study	*CPP Study*	*CPP Study*

October	November	December
New Hires	*New Hires*	*New Hires*
Security Academy	*Security Academy*	*Security Academy*
FTO	*FTO*	*FTO*
Basic Marksmanship	*Basic Marksmanship*	*Basic Marksmanship*
Existing Staff	*Existing Staff*	*Existing Staff*
Self Defense - Handcuffing	*Tactical Deployment*	*Firearms Qualification*
CPO Study	*CPO Study*	*CPO Study*
All Security Staff	*All Security Staff*	*All Security Staff*
		Live Fire Tactical
OC Spray Recert	*CPR/First Aid Recert*	*Deployment*
TDG Topic 10	*TDG Topic 11*	*TDG Topic 12*
Supervisors / Management	*Supervisors / Management*	*Supervisors / Management*
Required Reading	*Required Reading*	*Required Reading*
Conducting Evaluations	*Tactical Security Planning*	*Live Tactical Fire Range*
CPP Study	*CPP Study*	*CPP Study*

Figure 9.1   (*continued*)

155

TACTICAL DECISION GAMES

A favorite of mine are the TDGs. This form of training is easy to put together, can be promoted, and teach creativity and emotional intelligence while being a wonderful vehicle to remind your staff of critical policies and introduce new policies and legal matters.

TDGs are also a way to promote continuous training in your organization. All employees are given the initial training and in security, there are always required refresher courses. But what about the months in between? There is always time to train and TDGs can be quick training events which can be completed by email or during shift briefings.

TDGs are also taken from the military where small unit tactics are discussed and worked through to a successful ending. In small combat units, the topic can be how to take a defensive position using a squad with minimum logistics and no tactical assistance from air, artillery, or mortars. Add visual classroom assistance by using a sand table or topographical map, and a list of weapons, ammo, and other logistical small unit items. Now go. Let the team discuss and come up with a plan of attack in a set period. Right or wrong, the TDGs can teach subordinates how to lead, how to follow, how to read maps, define traps, select tactical advantages, and learn from others.

For your security team, you can put together similar scenario-based training. Maybe Gate 2 has fallen off the track so that shipping deliveries cannot pass through. The gate still needs guarding but another gate will need to be utilized for deliveries until Gate 2 is repaired. Your team shift has four patrol vehicles, one portable guard booth, and two extra programmable gate openers. How does the shift react? Let them come up with several different workarounds to the problem, knowing that two of your other gates cannot take tractor trailers and construction has trenched across the back road to Gate 12.

After the TDG, senior leadership needs to recognize the actions of the strong staff, those willing to work with others, those not participating, those who need additional training, and those with some positive skills while lacking other skills. TDGs are a great team-building and individual learning environment if done correctly.

A failure would be insulting to a subordinate in need of training in front of others. If the training is done improperly, the student only learns not to try. However, commenting that those in need of more training need to pay attention to the team member who did well in the scenario, or the military sense, and remind those who did well to explain how they came to the answers. Compliments are a strong motivator.

In the law enforcement world of training, the use of TDGs may have a different name but the benefits of practicing how to retain your weapon from different deadly attacks, or vehicle positioning in hot stops are all beneficial TDGs.

During a felony car stop, the subject's car is placed in a location that creates a hazard to the public, such as near a storefront or public building. Give the logistical limits of two marked units and a third coming from a long way off, a set number of uniformed officers, and maybe a K-9. The subject will not listen to commands shouted or over the loudspeaker, and go. Let the scenario play out and add injections to make the scenario more difficult as the training continues. Such as, one subject opens the passenger door and runs away from the vehicle and buildings.

A more complicated injection could be to add a supervisor to the scene where the law enforcement officers know what to do but are waiting to be told how the supervisors want them to act. Injecting recent events within the department or units can be seen as punitive if the previous actions are questioned, but it can also be used as a strong learning situation if handled correctly.

Within your organization, think of events that have taken place where the outcome was not perfect, or just not how management may have liked. Or an event that transpired in your industry or current events where your organization needs to ensure the staff member performs in a way that befits the customer service message of your department.

Another benefit of TDGs is that they can be used for small units, like a shift of officers, or down to how an individual reacts to an event. Using a TDG to see how a disparate group might work toward a correct tactical decision, based on each department's function or training can go a long way in preparing for potentially hazardous situations regarding weather, or other hazards. And, as might be obvious, TDGs can also be used to retrain your staff as to how your organization wants them to respond after an event.

Do you have a couple of ideas already? Knowing that in theoretical decisions, the resources can be innumerable but when setting up a TDG, within the objective, the resources should be limited. These resources should limit the time of day, number of staff, legal capabilities, and other issues.

How about a few simple TDG-suggested topics:

- Employee/customer/visitor forgets or loses their badge?
- A critical passageway will not open/close/lock? Or maintenance has blocked a critical walkway in your building.
- A customer's fingerprint will not read on a biometric reader.

- An unknown person is seen peering and taking photographs over your perimeter wall.
- An unknown person parks in front of your gate and blocks traffic. When security tries to ask them to move, the driver refuses to communicate with your staff.
- A badged relative attempts to remove a baby from the hospital ward to show another relative in the waiting room.
- A visitor has an emotional outburst in the main lobby.

For supervisors/managers, the TDGs can get more in-depth requiring a complex answer.

- An employee has filed a sexual or hostile harassment complaint against another employee.
- An employee has notified security that they have filed for a temporary restraining order regarding a domestic partner who has sworn to follow them to your workplace.
- A shift of officers has all tested positive for the latest viral outbreak.
- Cybersecurity gives notice that a security staffer has been attempting to gain access to file folders to which they do not have approved access. Or an unauthorized thumb drive has been introduced into one of the security computers.
- HR has sent a file to the wrong email address, causing twenty employees to receive salary information to which they should not have access.
- For hotel security staff – a guest has fallen in the shower and needs immediate first aid.
- An infant is walking around your parking lot crying.
- A contractor has been working in the hot sun all day and is seen staggering around the area in which he has been performing his tasks. He is not sweating and his face is very red.
- A person is trying to communicate with your security officer through sign language.

Take your pick of scenarios; however, ensure they are more than just an exercise for the sake of exercising. As with other training methods, the TDGs require fully documented objectives with a critical aspect to the objectives in how to determine a correct answer and analyze the decision methodology used to solve the given problem.

- Sometimes there is a low-cost training alternative to all of the above.

- This can be done in a small group of individually.
- Great way to remind staff of processes.
- Great way to require forethought of potentially disastrous events.
- A lesson guide must be developed to identify the objectives and outcomes.

Define the Need

Why is this training necessary for your department personnel? TDGs offer your department a method of training multiple subjects, since it is so different from other needs for training, you need to define why this method of training is needed. Topic refresher, critical taskings needing to be reviewed, critical thinking, small unit cohesive actions, you name the reason. In any training, the first step should be to draft a statement indicating the need to provide training for TDGs. It may also be advantageous to contact industry peers, law enforcement agencies, and other security professionals as to the usefulness of such training and incidents that would have benefitted from trained staff in this manner.

Conduct Task Analysis

The task analysis for TDGs should identify how and when the training method will be used.

The responses to the TDGs should direct your representatives in how to react to situations, specifically critical situations where different specifics change the actions of the employee. Check with your legal department to ensure the legalities of the actions.

Examples:

- You cannot tow a car with someone in it.
- Your staff must act with discretion when dealing with private matters such as a naked visitor who had fallen in the shower, or a domestic violence issue.

Develop Objectives

There are two ways to develop objectives for TDGs. One is to document that TDGs are a method of training and develop course objectives using TDGs as the overall goal. Or, as TDG is only a training methodology, each scenario will need its own set of objectives. It is important to recognize that TDGs are a great way to reinforce an existing body of applicable knowledge. Attempting to train criminal codes through TDGs will not work.

Therefore, enabling objectives should either cover how the TDGs will be used as a general training format or if critical enough, give the specifics of individual TDG courses. There are several training methods for this type of event, such as

- Live scenario-based
- Responding to a text-based scenario
- Live group activity
- Multiple department table-top exercises, or
- If the technology exists, manipulation of software or equipment to create an event where the staff must respond as previously trained.

How will the correct response be identified? What is considered a passing grade or successful accomplishment of the exercise? Will the training mentor or a trainer overseeing the scenario conduct an after-action review to identify faults and key points, or will incorrect responses be corrected during the scenario so that it can continue to its conclusion? These questions should be answered in the objectives.

Who can be considered a trainer or training mentor during the TDG? Identify a senior person to conduct the training by first explaining the exercise or scenario and the intended outcome. Using supervisory personnel in this way is a great method of growing your training staff.

Write the Curriculum

Every step of the course should be documented in the curriculum. This will allow for consistency in the training and especially practices and techniques. As there are various objectives and answers to scenarios, having one instructor teach a different response than another response to the syllabus has complications when used in the field.

Develop Testing

A formal test may not be necessary; however, ensuring all staff members understand the purpose of the TDG is necessary, even if the only purpose is to get staff to think outside the box during critical events. Some written

160

documentation that the TDG was completed and that each employee satisfactorily completed the TDG is critical for record-keeping and to ensure comprehension of your organization's requirement of each scenario.

REQUIRED READING

The security industry is changing with the society in which it performs. From new technologies, updated social norms, and relatively new business environments, those working in the security industry or having a security function need to be kept abreast of recent and evolving changes. Additional benefits of reading may include learning about different security roles and how they are diverse or similar to the current role, and better report writing.

The term security and the roles of security are considerably diverse, from an employee watching a parking lot during a football game to the installation of new access control, setting up new network protocols, designing crime prevention through environmental design (CPTED) into new building construction, conducting executive protection, or guarding the neonatal intensive care unit (NICU) in a hospital. The term security is widely diverse yet it has similarities that with creativity have cross-platform uses. Reading periodicals that discuss a variety of security concerns expands your employees' knowledge of the industry.

In a profession that requires report writing, reading proficiency, sentence and paragraph structure, basic knowledge of grammar, tense, and flow is important. With initial writing skills, reading has a positive impact toward better writing skills, if the reader pays attention to the writers' techniques in flow, tempo, and prose.

One of the budget-friendly benefits of required reading is that it is relatively inexpensive, may not require a lot of man-hours, and can increase the staff's professional knowledge in small parts. Secondly, some topics may be hard to teach in a lecture, such as the various forms of security.

Without breaching any copyright laws, getting permission to copy a magazine article or chapter in a book can get expensive. But, with digital documentation, simply sending a link to a site will minimize costs.

The required reading is not solely a military thing, but the military has taken it to a new level and brought it forward in today's digital world of short videos and headlines. For those unfamiliar, all branches of the

US military have lists of books that are required reading. The lists change based on rank, roles, and military branch. The intent is that it provides an expectation for what servicemembers should continue to learn. "The six objectives of the Marine Corps Professional Reading Program is to provide a continuum of study for all Marine leaders."

- To impart a sense of Marine values and traits.
- To increase knowledge of our profession.
- To improve analytical and reasoning skills.
- To increase the capacity of using printed media as a means of learning and communication.
- To increase knowledge of our nation's institutions and the principles upon which our country and way of life were founded.
- To increase knowledge of the world's governments, culture, and geography.

Paraphrasing from the Marine order regarding the Professional Reading Program:

> *The program serves as a bridge between an understanding of the organization, its environment, and the unique decision-making require-ments of tactical situations. Current events, characterized by threat and unforeseen requires leaders at all levels to make difficult and timely decisions amid complex and stressful situations. Repetitive and varying decision-making opportunities create competent judgment, flexibility, and adaptability. Field training and exercises are one means to improve thought processes; however, they may be limited in scope. Experience and knowledge offered in the required reading, if properly studied and understood serve as a knowledge multiplier.*

To put it in security words, security is widely diverse and more than actions and technology. It is a mindset, of well-thought processes that is based on historic events, and tactical and operational decisions. Repetition of operational requirements cements the necessary action but enhancing and creating opportunities through the reading of how others in security confront and deal with problems gives breadth and can improve the processes of customer service while still maintaining a high level of security.

Required reading can be as intense as your staff can accept. An article from a security publication may be a start but should be continued with readings regarding leadership, general management, business, threats both national or industry-specific, cybersecurity tactics, access control theory, or others. Or, assigning a chapter out of a book, or the whole book for that matter, can be as deep as your training requires.

You may see that the span of topics is as wide as you like. However, this is not just light reading, it has a purpose for your training efforts.

After reading the article determine the training value to your organization and the efforts of your staff. It can be minimal if the key idea in the article matches your needs. Identify the value of the article in a manner to document the training.

Define the Need

As identified above, the required reading still requires a formalized lesson plan with the objectives of each reading. Since the required reading is an individual learning experience, testing the learning objectives is necessary to ensure the staff members gather the necessary knowledge from the reading. One way to ensure the staff members gain the knowledge you wish them to gather is to use a student guide to be completed during the reading or provide the staff member with the list of objectives so that they are aware of what knowledge you wish them to gather.

Why is this training necessary for your department personnel? Or why is this training methodology/tactic something that your organization needs?

Answering the first question of why the staff needs the specific training from an article depends on the reading and will require a specific objective. However, if answering the second question in the continued use of the tactic to enhance and broaden the training experience given to your staff, then the objectives will be broad and only discuss the training tactic. For documentation purposes, leaning toward documenting the tactics has greater mobility and flexibility. For example, select twelve topics that your staff should have some knowledge of, then place these twelve topics in a calendar and rearrange them to fit your organizational needs. For example, every January you may want a reading that discusses flexibility in management to prepare for a policy change, or just before summer, an article discussing heat-related injuries.

Suggested Topics for Reading

The security professional gains experience through education and networking; however, there are some topics that due to your organization's posture or industry the staff member may never experience. One way of finding a place to start is by reviewing the list of subjects required for various security certifications.

The International Foundation of Protection Officer (IFPO)
Certified Protection Officer (CPO)
    Certified Security Supervision and Management (CSSM)

ASIS International
Associate Protection Professional (APP)
    Certified Protection Professional (CPP)
    Physical Security Professional (PSP)
    Professional Certified Investigator PCI

International Information System Security Certification Consortium (ISC2)
Certified Information Systems Security Professional (CISSP)

ISACA
Certified Information Systems Auditor
    Certified Information Systems Manager

Conduct Task Analysis

The task analysis for required reading should identify how and when the training method will be used. What is expected to be gained from the readings or the training tactics as a whole? Still, the exercise of documenting a task analysis proves the thought behind the use of the tactic as it is flexible, cost-effective, and continuous.

Develop Objectives

Developing a single course objective for required reading as a training event.
    Your objective should discuss the training tactic as a robust method of providing continuous training at all levels. Then follow up with individual objectives based on the readings. The flexibility will require updated objective development but may also become a library of topics that can be revisited should they be needed, such as critical thinking. The flexibility can also ensure your topics are timely regarding industry events or new threats as identified by others.

Developing a single course objective for each reading.

Should you decide on a more formalized set of objectives, then develop a course objective for each reading and a set of enabling objectives for each point your organization needs to ensure is covered and understood by the reader. This would be used for the reading of an entire text. There are several great textbooks that your organization can choose to further the knowledge of security practices, but few where the entire text needs to be a topic of immediate concern.

- If using a whole text, then each chapter could be used per month until completion.
- Many texts have a set of review questions at the end of each chapter, which could be used as a test to determine understanding.

Based on the education level or depth of the level of commitment to the profession, such would be a great way to force studying for one of the many available security certifications.

Write the Curriculum

Every step of the course should be documented in the curriculum. This will allow for consistency in the training and especially their practice and techniques. Each of your staff members will read and comprehend at various levels. Draft the courseware to recognize the ability of your staff and to ensure the objective of the reading assignment is met.

Develop Testing

Some written documentation that the required reading has been completed and the purpose of the reading has been attained through satisfactory comprehension is critical for the usefulness of the required reading. A test or maybe a short essay by the trainee to ensure comprehension can be adequate for record-keeping.

10

Supervisor and Manager Training

INTRODUCTION

Labels and terms such as supervisor, supervision, manager, management, leader, and leadership are too often bandied about with little thought to their meaning. From this text's point of view, let us mush them together to mean "boss." Unfortunately, too little training accompanies the title and role. Training the boss to be a leader or a manager usually takes back seat to training the staff, and supervisory training about security threats, new developments, and company needs. This section will highlight the differences between the terms, titles, positions, and roles each performs. Highlighted will be the recommended training curriculum to match the assignments.

In this text, the term supervisor and supervision will include security practitioners of all manners of security that have the responsibility to evaluate, give guidance, collect, receive, and conduct shift briefings, give shift assignments, ensure posts are relieved for breaks and lunches as needed, ensure reports and documents are correct before they are passed to management, and ensure the conduct of the shift is performing to standards.

Supervisors are not typically responsible for promotions, pay increases, hiring and firing personnel (though they may have input), budgets, strategic planning, systems design, enterprise risk, architectural

 DOI: 10.4324/9781003292586-13

security implementation and design, interfacing directly regarding planned human resources (HR), legal, operational department plans, or networking with law enforcement and government agencies.

A key function of security is that regardless of the field you are in, cyber, loss prevention, physical, systems installation, or design, and so on, security has the responsibility to identify, investigate, and notify people that they have breached your processes. Supervisors commend their subordinates for a good job and correct them when they make errors. Managers direct the department in correcting how they enforce policies. These are all higher level roles and necessitate great communication skills.

Regarding the terms manager and leader, there are differences. Few organizations need one or the other as they need managers to be leaders and leaders to be great managers. So, what is the difference?

In my research, it seems the experts also find it hard to define a leader and leadership. So, no matter what definition we come up with, there will be an argument over what may be missing.

In most cases, there are two types of leadership training, general and strategic. General leadership may be as simple as teaching the definitions of leadership qualities your organization has selected. Strategic leadership qualities that these traits have a specific need for your department. Being tactical has benefits for all leaders as their actions will follow a plan or pattern. Tactics in a security department may be seen as a more weighted quality when it comes to life safety or situational awareness.

Peter Drucker, famous for his theories X and Y of management, wrote that the only definition of a leader is someone who has followers. He also wrote that

> Leadership is not magnetic personality. That can be a glib tongue. It is not making friends and influencing people, that is flattery. Leadership is lifting a person's vision to a higher standard. The building of a personality beyond its normal limitations.

President and General Dwight D. Eisenhower opined that "Leadership is the art of getting someone else to do something you want done because he wants to do it."

Melting these two definitions, leadership is a grouping of qualities that gives reason for followers to act and perform in a certain way. We can only hope that the person with leadership qualities leads for the right reasons. Ken Blanchard added the term "servant leadership" since as an employee of an organization in a leadership role, those qualities are used to "obtain the organization's objectives." In our training purpose, this may be more pointedly correct.

If these are the definitions of leadership, then what is management? Similarly, the research proves to have a varied set of definitions, including trickery and deceit. In a basic form, management is the process of organizing, controlling, and administrating an effort. In your organization, it can be anything from finances, logistics, personnel, and services.

Within your organization, I assume you want a supervisor who can lead others within the scope and for which that person is hired. That supervisor may have minor management duties such as time-keeping administration, shift assignments, and ensuring the staff has adequate equipment for the position.

What are the qualities that require training to necessitate this leader? And which qualities should your training include to maximize that leader's growth potential and ultimate value in your organization?

WHY WE TRAIN

At the beginning of the book, Why We Train was discussed. Those reasons were pointed toward supervision, leadership, and management more so than at the entry level for security practitioners. To review why we train (Section 1, Chapter 1).

Personal Reason

Training is an expression of self and self-growth. You train yourself so that you can answer the big questions when the time comes. Your growth through training should induce your staff to also continue to self-educate and learn the trade of security.

- You need to keep up with your profession and craft.
- You need to educate yourself about the industry in which your organization performs.
- You need to be ready for change.
- You need flexibility.
- Your self-training regimen should be viewed by your subordinates as the norm.

Personnel

You should consider your staff as your family, comrades, and even friends. Training your staff is your sole duty as their guardian, leader, or friend.

- The obvious reason is to train them to do their job.
- Training is required.
- When all your staff have entered their position with the same training baseline, they become a member of the team.
- The continuous training that builds on prior training gives proof of a future in the profession and within the organization.
- If we consider security as a paramilitary role, then being mission-oriented gives cause and motivation to employees.
- Staff retention.

Organization

Training is a wonderful benefit to the entire organization in which you are employed. It benefits from the training you provide your representatives.

- A trained staff is more cost-effective.
- A trained staff is more efficient.
- Your organization has its own way of doing things.
- Every organization hopes to have a group of departments performing in an orchestrated fashion that promotes efficiency and the company's vision.
- A motivated and well-trained security department allows for confidence at the executive level.
- Security as a sales tool is a follow-on to the item above.
- Here is one for HR – a trained staff, a staff that expects continuous training and education will have less turnover.

Legal

At some point in your career, the actions of your subordinates or team members will come into question. Whether the question comes from an employee, customer, executive, or other parties, you owe it to yourself, the company, your profession, and subordinates to be able to prove the validity of the training delivered, training received, and training competency and knowledge retention through documentation and references.

You will need to prove that the training administered was well-researched, fully documented, and professionally delivered. And that the student understood the material and at the time of the training could use the training successfully. If the training is poor in any of the above attributes, then retraining is necessary and should be done at a cyclic rate as identified through your research.

- Marksmanship is a diminishing skill that requires constant practice. The hand–eye coordination of safely drawing the weapon, aim point, and breathing control all while thinking of what is beyond the target and the employee's safety requires constant and regular retraining and practice. This and other subjects need to be researched as to the frequency of training.

Profession

Though people in our profession save lives, protect the untold value of assets, and perform professionally every hour of every day, the general public does not always see security as having great value. Poorly trained and equipped personnel harm our professional reputation.

- Your staff is the future of the profession. Every course they attend prepares them for the day they take over as a site supervisor, crisis manager, or take up other management roles.
- Promoting your profession includes promoting the efforts of your fellow security professionals and your staff who work toward certification, attend training events, and perform in an exemplary fashion.

Failure

We all make mistakes. What level of mistake are you willing to accept from your people?

- Train so that your staff does not make mistakes.
- Train so that when mistakes are made, the correct quick reaction fixes the problem.
- Through training, you can put processes in place to counter the possibility of failure.

- Failure, though not a pleasant topic, is a key reason to have available a sound and comprehensive training syllabus for your staff and organization.
- All resiliency processes have a substantial failure identification and training component to compensate for failures.

ORGANIZATIONAL REQUIREMENTS

Your organization should have position descriptions that list the prerequisites for each position. Conducting a review to ensure your department equally fits within your organization's structure is important. Imagine that the position of "Accountant II" requires a specific college degree in accounting but directors within that department do not. That an Accountant II position requires specific knowledge that their supervisors and leader do not makes little sense. What knowledge or experiences do you require that can be equal to a four-year college degree? Or should you require a college degree in criminal justice or homeland security for some positions?

Reviewing the position descriptions for your department may be necessary to ensure your department requirements for all positions meet an industry standard, are ethical, unbiased, that ample candidates for the position are available in the area, and that the position description befits what you want of your department. If these qualities or experiences are necessary for the position, then a refresher or more in-depth training in those areas should also be necessary.

With the goal of this training to fit your organizational goals, this is a great time to include other department personnel in the training. Knowing what the other departments and their personnel do for the organization and how those offerings complete the product offering of the organization is a growth multiplier. Giving value to the other department personnel may provide your supervisors with a better understanding of why a security practice is necessary as well as allow them to understand the practice as a benefit and not an impediment.

SECURITY INDUSTRY STANDARD

One standard that you want to review is the International Foundation of Security Officers (IFPO), Certified in Security Supervision and

Management (CSSM). IFPO has tailored distance-learning courseware that meets the needs of general security supervisors and managers. The course curriculum shows IFPOs' depth of knowledge necessary for a security officer to rise through the ranks of the profession. The IFPO CSSM standard is rising in acceptance and global recognition.

The course takers log into a video server for courses as well as receive the text *Security Supervision: Theory and Practice of Asset Protection* (Fourth Edition) published by this publisher, which covers the below list of topics. There is a mid-term examination, a proctored final examination of over 250 questions, and finally a written essay.

Topics included in the courseware:

Future of private security	Security personnel selection
Motivation and evaluation	Security officer scheduling
Interpersonal communications	Staff training and development
Company policies and procedures	Testimony in court
Managing/supervising to reduce liability	Risk and crisis management
Statistical analysis	Investigations
Legal aspects of security	Sexual harassment
Security medical response	Designing operations centers
Security technologies	Workplace violence
Crime prevention/community relations	Supervisor's role in training
Testing for learning retention	

ASIS International has both the Associate Protection Professional (APP) and the Certified Protection Professional (CPP). The APP knowledge base is a portion of the CPP knowledge base and the base requirement for security management or supervision experience is fewer years than the minimum requirement for the CPP.

Both the APP and CPP bodies of knowledge are taken from the *Protection of Assets Manual* published by ASIS International and five additional standards, two of which are ANSI Standards and are also published by ASIS International.

The APP is touted by ASIS as the "first rung" of a security manager's career ladder. The requirement for security management experience is one to four years or a combination of security management experience and college degrees.

The curriculum consists of four domains:

Security Fundamentals   Business Operations
Risk Management   Response Management

The ASIS International CPP Standard has been considered the pinnacle of security management certification for as long as I can remember. It is globally recognized and has great value in our industry.

Eligibility for this certification requires nine years in security and at least three years having been the "responsible charge of a security function." (See the chapter on Security Manager/Director for more on the CPP Certification.)

SUPERVISORY TRAINING

As there is a difference between leadership and management training, I would first recommend focusing on supervisor or leadership training. Your organization may want to conduct leadership and management training within the same curriculum; however, for this text, we will separate the two.

You should know that numerous companies perform such training. Many have developed a curriculum that may fit your organizational needs, and most of these companies understand the need to slightly customize the course to fit your organizational requirements.

Define the Need

To start determining what necessary training your organization's supervisors require, create a formalized lesson plan with objectives and testing of the learning objectives to ensure the trainees have gained from the course. One way to ensure the staff member gains the knowledge you wish them to gather is to use a student guide to be completed during the course or provide the staff member with the list of objectives so that they are aware of what knowledge you wish them to gather.

Why is this training necessary for your department personnel? Or why is this training something that your organization needs? And, what topics should be taught in your leadership course? These questions should invoke a larger question within your organization – what qualities, traits, or principles of a leader does your organization want for their supervisors? From a general point of view, the leadership traits that your organization espouses are important to document, list, advertise, and profess.

Societal changes, demographics, and cultural differences are three reasons that you want to provide leadership training. How a person perceives leadership from what they have seen on television shows, what they have experienced with parental methods, what they have experienced in their neighborhood colloquialisms, or other past events may not be the leadership qualities that your organization wants of their leaders. Yelling, taking away privileges, striking someone, belittling subordinates, or bullying may be how your staff members were raised or what they commonly identify as common leadership methods. Parents, teachers, and even supervisors rarely receive training in how to lead. Your department and organization deserve better.

If your organization does not have a documented listing of the leadership qualities that a supervisor should be taught, it is a great place to start. Each branch of the US military has a list of qualities, and several books on the subject that might prove helpful. The Marine Corps has 14 Leadership Traits and 11 Leadership Principles (MC-RP0103).

US Marine Corps Leadership Traits:

- Justice: Know the rules, obey them, and reward and enforce them consistently and fairly.
- Judgment: Weigh the facts and potential courses of action to make sound choices.
- Dependability: Certainty that assignments will be performed correctly.
- Initiative: Taking action, when necessary, in the absence of higher supervision.
- Decisiveness: Ability to make decisions after considering the circumstances.
- Tact: Dealing with situations with courtesy.
- Integrity: Act with a moral principled character.
- Enthusiasm: Sincere interest in the performance of duties.
- Endurance: Performance with mental and physical stamina.
- Bearing: Creating a favorable image through carriage, appearance, and performance.
- Unselfishness: Your team's comfort and need comes first.
- Courage: Mental quality that recognizes fear of danger but proceeds with calm firmness.

- Knowledge: To lead, you must know your job.
- Loyalty: Faithfulness to your organization and team members.

US Marine Corps Leadership Principles:

- Know yourself and seek self-improvement
- Be technically and tactically proficient
- Know your people and look out for their welfare
- Keep your personnel informed
- Set the example
- Ensure that the task is understood, supervised, and accomplished
- Train as a team
- Make sound and timely decisions
- Develop a sense of responsibility among your subordinates
- Employ your command within its capabilities
- Seek responsibilities and take responsibility

The US Army's Leadership development is split between Attributes and Competencies (Army Reg 600-100 dated April 5, 2017).

Attributes

- Character – values, empathy, service ethos, discipline
- Presence – bearing, fitness, confidence, resilience
- Intellect – mental agility, judgment, innovation, tact, expertise

Competencies

- Leads – others, builds trust, extends influence, leads by example, communicates
- Develops – positive environment, prepares self, develops others, stewards the profession
- Achieves – gets results

From my experience in the military, law enforcement, and commercial business, here are a few of the leadership qualities and realities that I have come to recognize.

- Leaders must be visionary. Have a strong vision for the environment and their team's efforts within that vision. This requires a complete knowledge of the tasks at hand, an open vision toward threats, risks, and changes that will come, and a sense of what to do during those trying times.

- Leaders must have integrity and ethical values. The first time a team member catches the leader in a lie or takes credit for something they did not do; all trust is lost. Leaders must have a strong ethical responsibility to deal with customers, their subordinates, and their peers. Trust is critical when initiating actions to stop a threat or evolving event. We all make mistakes, so being able to apologize and right any wrong you may have done also goes a long way to mend trust when you do make that error.
- Leaders must develop and use power. Power comes from within and most commonly comes from the respect deserved for being a true leader. After that power is earned through merit, the leader must learn to use that power to better the team and the organization.
- Leaders must be accountable and responsible. Leaders must hold themselves accountable as well as their subordinates. A mistake can look bad, but hiding a mistake or not taking accountability for that mistake is worse as it breaches your team's and management's trust. Take responsibility for your team and give credit when due.
- Leaders must be tough and resilient. Being a leader is not always easy, and it can be very hard if that new supervisor comes up through the ranks with the staff that he or she now leads. Leaders must be level-headed, firm, fair, and capable of change.

Some of the outdated leadership principles are:

- Expert-based power as a primary leadership quality. Just because someone knows the rule book does not in itself make a great leader.
- Incentive power, threat power, and organizational power. Giving gifts for someone to do as they are instructed, threatening that same person if they do not, or using the organization as the scapegoat for why a subordinate needs to act.
- Parent-child communications or lack of communication altogether. Treat your subordinates as equals. Do not talk down to them and explain the reasons why. Adults want to know why more than a child does. Explaining the "why" allows an adult to place purpose to their task.
- Overuse emails instead of talking to your subordinates. Emails have their place when communicating to a large group or when speed is

important to a large group. But, hiding behind an email to pass bad news without having to face your staff is not ethical treatment. Whenever possible, talking directly with your staff is critical.

- Rash and unexplained decisions are paralyzing to the team as it does not give them time to prepare, and their flexibility is strained. It also makes your subordinates wait for the next order instead of using self-motivation.
- Being moody and unpredictable is cancer to any team as it eats away at the willingness of your subordinates to approach you. When your staff does not know which personality you are bringing to work today, it will destroy a productive team.
- Assuming the factors that motivate you are the same motivators as your subordinates may work in the short term but will lack long-term fulfillment.
- Your greatest goal is staying within budget. The budget may be one of your responsibilities, but it is not your subordinate's.
- Providing only corrective or negative feedback. Yes, correction is a responsibility of a leader but so is seeing the great work your team completes.
- Having all the answers or making all the decisions removes self-initiative from your subordinates and does not allow them to grow with their ideas on how to solve problems. Listen to your staff and yes, they may stumble with their ideas, but so did you. It is part of growing.

You should have a good starting point to determine the need to provide supervisor training in leadership.

After defining your organization's need to provide leadership training to the subordinates with identified leadership qualities, you may want to identify a method of training each quality. After listening to a lecture on these qualities, and the telling of historical stories to cement the ideas, practice is required. Perhaps pair the students to act out a scene with another student supervising the interaction. The more they hear the principles applied, they will start to recognize the method your organization wants them to use.

After the definition, discuss the benefits of a leader with that characteristic and the problem when a leader does not have that quality. Using stories and examples in recent news, without using controversial issues, is a good way to give the staff members the ability to retain the information and have a greater understanding.

Conduct Task Analysis

The task analysis for leadership or supervisor training should identify how and when the training method will be used. What is expected to be gained from the training as a whole? The exercise of documenting a task analysis proves the thought behind the use of the tactic as it is flexible, cost-effective, and continuous. If your organization has a training department, coordinating your efforts in leadership training goes a long way, both budgetary and for the organization's growth. Or consider reaching out to other departments, such as HR regarding what should be taught and how. Including HR may increase your budgetary dollars and time when including other departments in such training.

Develop Objectives

Develop an overall course objective based on the findings of your analysis and list of traits. Ensure the course objective defines the benefit to the organization and any broad-stroke measuring tools to ensure the course has value.

You should assume this course will have multiple sessions and various depths for such a diverse subject. Your course may start with an evaluation of the students to determine where their personalities lie and what are their strengths and weaknesses. Then start with a few lessons on the different criteria to recognize where a team member may be in the personality spectrum. Then use this knowledge of others' weaknesses and strengths as a team-building benefit. Another benefit is that your new supervisors will learn how to communicate best with a person based on their personality.

Examining the current personality of your staff members has many benefits. It is good that your staff is comprised of a multitude of personalities. The more personalities, the greater the roundness of your staff. Each of your staff members probably has a little of all the personality categories but typically there will be a dominant trait. The more dominant a single personality trait, the more important it is to make sure the other traits are developed.

To identify the personalities of your staff, there are several person-ality tools. There will be a cost associated with using one of these tools, but the benefits far outweigh the cost. When selecting a tool, look for tools that are widely accepted by the industry, have longevity, and have verified results. These tools may also require that the personality survey be sent to a certified assessor. This external assessment is beneficial as it should remove any perceived or potential problems, such as personal prejudices and a poor assessment of the survey results.

Coursework should be written to understand and give examples of how to recognize mental health issues, handle claims of harassment, workers' compensation issues, in-depth soft-skill training, legalities of conducting new hire interviews, and formatting weekly, monthly, and annual goal reports, and other organizational specific functions that supervisors are required to know and perform.

Having a multi-session course in leadership will require multiple terminal objectives with enabling objectives working toward the completion. Your objectives should discuss the desired outcome of the training and all the benefits to the employee. You may also point out that if an employee is a candidate for a promotion, having this training is required within a set number of days. Giving the new supervisor all the tools, they need to succeed minimizes the anxiety of a new position.

Should an outside company be brought in to conduct this training, ensure administrative requirements such as copyright privileges and additional cost of personality evaluations are called out. Using outside sources shows that a collegian-level educator conducting the training is a benefit to their new position. The outside source also can bring certified methodologies such as identifying the supervisory style of the current trainees and what subjects need to be stressed to enhance some behaviors.

Write the Curriculum

Every step of the course should be documented in the curriculum. This will allow for consistency in the training and especially practice and techniques. Each of your new supervisors should be able to understand the course and be able to comprehend and put the new knowledge to use. Draft the courseware to recognize the ability of your staff and to ensure the objective of assignments is satisfactory to the criteria you have set.

Develop Testing

This course should be considered advanced training. Since being able to communicate well is a goal of leadership, having oral report assignments with presentation materials, and written reports of a few of the subjects are warranted.

Should you have a candidate who cannot communicate well due to fear, this person may need more training to overcome the obstacle and promotion may be delayed in accordance.

Train the Trainer

In several of the above training subjects, the person who will conduct the training and deliver the information is probably organic, and from within your security team members who has the expertise and capabilities to impart the knowledge in the method and time available. With little thought, it should be recognized that those who provide the training should be instructed on how to train. This course topic can be internal training but the list of traits the trainer should have and profess should be documented and reviewed periodically while the instructor provides a training lesson.

Like with all training, define the need, conduct a task analysis, develop the objectives, write the course, and then test the trainees. The one additional component to ensure continued compliance is to conduct periodic re-evaluations of the trainer.

There are several benefits to your training staff being organic.

- The trainer assists in the continued culture of training. Well after the training event, the trainer will rejoin the security staff and be able to correct or assist in complicated events.
- There are some cost savings for a shift supervisor or manager conducting the training while on shift.
- The supervisor conducting the training and being recognized as the subject matter expert will follow your operational methods and not allow staff to cut corners in the field.
- Being recognized as the subject matter expert and trainer in a subject is internally motivating for the person you have assigned to give the training.
- If several of your supervisors are trained as trainers, then the organization has a built-in redundancy when one is not available to conduct training.
- Shuffling the training in a drawn-out course such as an academy is beneficial for the students to combat boredom and change up the delivery style, stories, and experiences.

It may be human nature to look for shortcuts and put more emphasis on a favorite subject and spend less time or less emphasis on a lesson that the trainer finds unfavorable or not one of their strengths. If this occurs in your training, those staff members taught by that trainer will typically have the same weakness for that subject. One way to mitigate the possibility that a trainer may minimize a lesson is to review their performance by sitting in on that class, witnessing the trainee's perform-ance in this subject, and reviewing the trainee's evaluation of the instruction.

To ensure your training staff is performing well, consider these options:

- With a well-developed curriculum, a benefit is that any of your trained trainers should be able to pick up the curriculum and teach the course. If a lesson topic guide is used, there should be no missed information or any lost critical components or knowledge. The better prepared and knowledgeable the instructor is with the course material, the more complete the material and topics will be presented.
- Video your subject matter expert instructing the topic and allow the instructor to play the video during subsequent training classes. It is recommended that this tactic only be used for short course subjects. This is a great method to ensure every staff member gets the same training.
- Conduct a performance analysis of students to see if one class performs better than another as a whole course or just in certain subjects.
- Periodically, have a senior instructor or manager sit in to evaluate the instructor's performance, communication style, speed, and completeness of the course materials. Every instructor should be evaluated periodically to ensure they are performing in the manner your organization wants and demands. Evaluations should never be seen as negative or more cumber-some than any other session. If it is considered negative, there will be a problem with what the organization expects versus what is being commonly performed.

There is only one course specific for the training of security trainers, of which I am aware. The International Foundation for Protection Officers (IFPO) has a certification for Certified Protection Officer Instructors (CPOI). The requirements to attain the CPOI are not slight but also not so heady as to be unattainable. There is a requirement to have five years of teaching experience. However, IFPO offers a train-the-security-trainer course that can assist with this requirement.

There is one very valid benefit of having a few of your training staff become CPOI in that it allows those to proctor the Certified Protection Officer (CPO) test. Should your department wish for your staff to obtain the CPO designation, having a CPOI on staff is valuable.

Trainer Selection

Generally, all supervisors should be capable of being a trainer. This is inherent as a primary supervisory task is ensuring their subordinates know their job and if they do not, then the supervisor needs to conduct the training to get the employee to perform the task adequately while continually conducting oversight. The training continues until the supervisor has a comfort level that the employee can do the same task time and time again with less supervision at the same level of correctness.

Being a trainer, however, does require a few specific characteristics.

- Leadership – the trainer is the leader of the classroom. Being able to supervise and oversee the conduct of students while still conveying the material is important. Some materials, such as self-defense, or de-escalation practices may cause inappropriate behavior or conversation and will require a strong leader to train while preventing or stopping inappropriate activity.
  - The necessary touching of another person to practice hand-cuffing can result in injury or possible inappropriate touching.
  - De-escalation practices can lead to off-color comments. Use of bad language and name-calling may be common in the field but should not be allowed in the classroom.
  - All weapons training is inherently dangerous if not super-vised closely and can lead to the injury of an attendee.
  - The trainer must be able to command the classroom, for time management and complete coverage of the course material. I would guess you have been to a training session where a break was given by the instructor but the attendees did not return in time and the class was delayed. If something similar happens during your training events, it demonstrates poor adherence to the rules set by the trainer or the respect of the attendees for the trainer.
  - Movies are made about high school classrooms in disarray due to a student not respecting the teacher, in your training

events, the leader cannot allow a similar situation. And, if anything of the kind does occur, the attendees need to be counseled and, depending on the action, determine if their employment with the company will continue.

- Knowledge of the material – your trainees should be able to consider the trainer as the subject matter expert and that the knowledge delivered will include new information and anecdotal stories to assist in their comprehension of the concept or topics.
  - Often when attending a training event, the instructor or speaker first introduces themselves, and that introductory statement tells the attendees why the instructor should be giving the course and why the attendees should listen.
- Clear voice and language – if the trainer is speaking to the attendees and their only method of learning is by listening to the instructor, that instructor's voice and language must be capable of conveying the information.
  - Imagine a firearms range instructor who does not speak loud enough to be heard over the noise of an active range, range attendees wearing aural protection, or unclear commands due to poor language skills causing shooters to be confused as to the specifics of the course of fire, to include rate or number of shots.
  - Note that when shooters cannot understand or hear the instructor, their attention is drawn away from marksmanship and safety.
- Patience and consideration – not all trainees will pick up skills as easily as others. This does not allow for the instructor to bypass a section of the training or to accept the limitation, it requires the trainer to patiently continue to train that trainee until the skill is completed correctly with some regularity.
  - It may be easy to recognize that some trainees with limitations do not have the needed skills and capabilities. This is the wrong mindset. A good trainer can think outside the box and find alternate capabilities that allow the trainee to succeed.
- Strategic and organized – a trainer must have a clear strategic method of training. The more complicated a concept that is being trained, the trainer needs a greater ability to break the complication into smaller parts that grow and complement the prior part

toward a constructed final product or concept. Complicated concepts can be bodily movements during handcuffing and marksmanship, can be developing the elements of a crime, or can be a fast-paced deduction of a concept like the use of force continuum.

- Analyze, improve, and have flexibility – For the most part, training is a cost center. Training costs money and time and does not make a direct profit. This fact should be recognized by the training and allow the trainer to find trends and technology that reduce and improve the cost of the training as well as compre-hension of the material.
- As change is the only constant in life, the trainer must be flexible enough to use new training trends and recognize that the change is intended to increase productivity and that comprehension is good for the student and organization.
- Most have grown up sitting in lecture after lecture, walking out with much less than 10% of the knowledge provided during the event. A lecture is considered passive learning, where the student just sits and listens, sometimes taking notes or asking questions. Changing or adding exercises, handouts, memorable quips, sound bites, videos, or other training injections to increase the takeaway knowledge and thereby comprehension is the goal.
- Training requires considerable administration and curriculum development. Making changes in the curriculum and docu-menting those changes is crucial to your training efforts.
  - A small, but critical change in the course causes modifications to be made in the lesson topic guide, the objectives, the student guide, and testing.
  - Critical to documenting changes is analyzing why the change is necessary.

Define the Need

As your department provides training to staff members, it should be easy to identify that those providing the training should receive instruction on training methodologies. The training event is a process that starts with the instructor being prepared for the course. This requires knowledge of the subject, attitude toward training, and the extra assignment of training, combined with a skills workshop to ensure the communication style, speed, and delivery are fitting your workforce.

Conduct a Task Analysis

Numerous topics could be taught in a train-the-trainer course. Many more than just ensuring the trainer candidate knows the material. During your analysis, you will need to determine which topics you find necessary to ensure your training staff is comfortable.

If your organization already has a formal training department, they may be able to assist with providing this training for your trainers. However, if the organization does not have one, and they provide training to other departments, you may want to recommend and share duties to ensure all trainers in the organization receive the same training.

Here are a few topics your trainers may need and should be in your course:

- The difference between training and education
- The roles of the instructor as a trainer, facilitator, and supervisor
- The needs of those being trained
- The training pyramid from passive to active learning (lecture, discussion, hands-on, practice, and testing)
- Classroom layout styles and benefits and limitations of each
- Use of visual aids and over-use of visual aids
- Encouraging and managing discussion and questions
- Handling interruptions, challenges, solutions, and workarounds
- Managing sensitive issues and ethics in the classroom
- Time schedules, breaks, and self-study periods
- Evaluating the student's abilities
- Public speaking
- Organizational defined policies

Train-the-trainer instruction and coursework can be outsourced. If your research concludes that the use of a contractor to provide the coursework and/or the instruction of the course, ensure organizational acceptance of the topics and modify as necessary for your needs.

A legal review is recommended to identify ownership of the source materials' copywrite status and the capabilities of copying materials, modifications to topics, and key teaching points.

Develop the Objectives

Train-the-trainer courses are typically several days in length as each student participates and then completes short instructional drills. An overall course objective should provide broad strokes as to the purpose of the course and its benefits to the organization.

Based on your task analysis and organizational approval, develop the topics in a smooth flow and develop objectives accordingly so that objectives overlap and build toward a conclusion of skills and knowledge.

Lastly, how will the objectives be tested to ensure the students have reached comprehension and have the ability to put the new knowledge to use? Develop multiple testing initiatives that befit the objectives as well as teach the varied testing methods.

Define the Training Form

How will this training be delivered? The lecture is a component, but the use of discussion, small team tasks, and lesson practice will allow for the classroom to be re-arranged several times to prove the benefits of each in accordance with the training topics.

Write the Curriculum

Every step of the course should be documented in the curriculum. This will allow for consistency in the training and especially the staff's practice and delivery techniques. Each of those learning-to-be trainers should be able to understand and comprehend the course objectives and put the new knowledge to use.

Draft the courseware to recognize the ability of your staff and to ensure the objective of assignments is satisfactory to the criteria you have set.

Develop Testing

This course should be considered advanced training. Being able to communicate well, tackle tough classroom discussions, and maintain a controlled classroom while still promoting open discussions requires training and practice. Therefore, the testing of the students will be multi-faceted.

Simple exams, written works, development of trainer evaluation criteria, and form should be created for later use. A recommendation is for the class to evaluate the practice instruction, so the students learn what criteria are being looked at and what constitutes acceptable performance.

EVENT MANAGEMENT

Most organizations, periodically, have events that are out of the ordinary and require a concerted effort between multiple departments. The event can be a tour by a local college, HR having testing for multiple positions, a group of operational auditors, a political or celebrity visit, or a sales visit to your space that is being used as a training event. When the normal operations are either stilted for the event or normal operations continue concurrent with the event, regardless of daily tempo, this additional coordination by security personnel is common and requires additional training.

Flexibility is the key to successfully ensuring security personnel are used efficiently and that the event does not cause an undue risk or security compromise.

Managing an event that requires coordination with other departments is a considerable skill. Leaning on existing skill sets, identifying desirable outcomes, and dealing with unexpected delays are just a few of the important event management concepts. Training supervisors reacting in a manner prescribed by your organization during the event is important to ensure the safety of personnel, and the continued protection of the organization.

The definition of an event is something that is a little out of the ordinary from your organization's daily activities. If these events become more commonplace, a procedure can be documented that would make them less of an event but still a great training ground for a new supervisor to act.

Define the Need

This training should be geared toward supervisory personnel in how to handle such an event, how to assist in the planning, what is expected of security, and the continued security of the facility and its personnel. The criticality of event timing and the need for security to be flexible when timetables lag or are hurried is important.

As your department is providing training to staff members, it should be easy to identify that those providing the training should have experience with your organization and how events are handled, the purpose of the event, and any contingencies that need to be prepared.

Conduct a Task Analysis

What special events have you recently had at your facilities? This is a good place to start because any hurdles that need to be negotiated are fresh in your staff and the organization's mind.

List the events and anything that could have been done better.

Here are a handful of items that your training may want to cover:

- Parking and traffic flow, barriers, and shuttle service. With numerous guests coming to a meeting at your facility at the same time, parking may become an issue, as well as a continued avenue of approach for normal daily traffic.
- Facility access and badging or ensuring guests have been identified. Will guests be required to receive visitor badges; what forms of identification will be accepted or how will you verify the identity of guests in your facility?
- Use of closed areas and emergency egress doors may be required for guest movement, catering, or workaround for operational staff to not conflict with the event.
- Signage is important to allow guests to move around public areas without the need for continuous assistance. For instance, which way are the bathrooms, smoking areas, or quiet spaces for receiving phone calls?
- Are restrooms available in substantial numbers based on the number of guests or will restrooms in other areas need to be made available?
- What is the event's purpose, what are the high points of the visit, and what special areas are necessary to be accessed?
- Locus of control for escorting personnel. If groups of visitors are to be escorted in special areas, how many guests can be escorted by a single person while maintaining control of their movements?
- Will food and beverages be served and what arrangements are necessary for catering and food preparation?
- Housekeeping and trash removal are necessary should food be made available and, as the meeting continues after the lunch period, to keep odors to a minimum.
- Special table or desk arrangement. If the standard conference room is not suitable for the meeting setup, rooms with movable table arrangements require prior setup with adequate seating.

- Audiovisual (AV) equipment and personnel on standby as what training event occurs without an AV problem.
- Safety in the tour or walking areas.
- Cyber security for any removable media. If a computer belonging to your organization is used for presentations, and the presentation is brought on a thumb drive or sent in an email, allow cyber to scan the files for malware.
- Pre-event coordination. Your department should have a representative at any pre-event coordination meeting to plan for adequate staffing.
- Post-event findings and discussions are a good way to learn from issues that arose during the event. Remember to ask all your staff for knowledge of any complaint or suggestions from one of the guests.
- Threat assessment. Every person who enters your facility is a threat. They are walking out with more information than they came in with. Model the event to ensure protection from threats.
- Is a non-disclosure form necessary? If the event releases company private, proprietary, or competitive data, legal should require a non-disclosure agreement (NDA) to be signed in advance of the event. Also, have a plan for what to do when a person in the meeting refuses to sign the NDA. Or when collecting the signed NDA, it has been signed with a fictitious name.
- Review and approve any handouts or takeaways. Depending on the level of the meeting, marketing, legal, and operational departments should review any material to be removed from the facility for confidential items. Standardized and pre-printed materials are recommended.
- Exiting the facility, badge return. When the guests depart the facility should the badges be collected, are all guests accounted for to ensure there are no stay-behinds such as someone using the restroom or a surreptitious lingerer.

You may be able to discern that if such events are commonplace in your facilities, then a policy and set procedures may be needed.

Develop the Objectives

A course on event management should probably be a single class indicating a single course objective that also serves as the terminal objective.

The number of your enabling objectives will depend on the grouping of the above tasks and how in-depth your department's involvement will be in the event planning and coordination.

Based on your task analysis and organizational approval, develop the topics in a smooth flow and develop objectives accordingly so that objectives overlap and build toward a conclusion of skills and knowledge.

Lastly, how will the objectives be tested to ensure the students have reached comprehension and the ability to put the new knowledge to use? In this case, testing initiatives may be a practice with supervision to ensure compliance with the objectives.

Define the Training Form

As this can be a short course of just a single class, it will probably be suitable for a lecture or discussion format.

Write the Curriculum

Every step of the course should be documented in the curriculum. This will allow for consistency in the training and especially the staff's practice and delivery techniques. Each of those responsible for oversight of a special event should be able to understand and comprehend the course objectives and put the new knowledge to use.

Draft the courseware to recognize the responsibilities, and abilities of your staff, and to ensure the objective of assignments is satisfactory to the criteria you have set.

Develop Testing

This course could be considered advanced or supervisory training. Those in this training should be able to communicate well, tackle tough discussions, and maintain flexibility while being able to make quick decisions based on organizational standards. Therefore, the testing of those in this training may be multi-faceted or simply conduct a live event and have supervision assist.

Simple exams may be necessary to ensure adherence to policies and procedures.

CRISIS MANAGEMENT

In any organization, crisis management and crisis response are immensely important skills. And every time we read the newspaper or turn on the television, there is more proof that having a crisis management plan and training for that plan is vital. It is so important that many operational audits require formal and ongoing crisis management plans and training. Depending on the operation, environment, and size of the organization, the more complicated and serious the skills become.

A crisis can be considered any event that is outside the normal operation, that is unexpected and requires more skills, equipment, and manpower than usual. The level of crisis may depend on the criticality of your operations, the surprise, unexpectedness, and unpreparedness for the event. The effect is that the organization's survivability may be at stake or that lives are in jeopardy.

A crisis can be categorized as:

- Financial: Depending on the type of organization to which you are employed, a financial crisis may not be a form of crisis you will incur, like if you work for a government agency. However, if you work in a commercial organization, the sudden loss of revenue due to losing market share or sudden trend change can jeopardize the ability to purchase, pay employees, or provide customers with products or services.

  In your role as security, these issues would affect your department but not as much in the planning or training for such an event.

- Technology: This type of crisis is all over the news, with malware, viruses, or hacking remaining constant threats, but also hardware malfunctions. Having an experienced cyber security team and considerable backup processes is critical but still not all saving.

  A technology crisis can also include building systems such as heating, ventilation, and air conditioning (HVAC). Sending staff home because the building is not safe due to heat or cold causes a strain on productivity in manufacturing or the ability to provide services to your customers.

  The inoperability of other infrastructure also fits into this category. Should your facilities or a portion of your facilities lose power, identifying a cause and its reclamation can be lengthy. And regardless of your organization's ability to self-generate power, fuel has been an issue in longer-term crises. After several of the large storms that hit America, the ability to maintain fuel for generators was in some cases, non-existent.

- Personnel: If a member of the organizational staff becomes involved in criminal or unethical actions, your organization's reputation can suffer if it becomes widespread to the public. Word travels fast and customers learn of incidents faster than management can react.

    In recent public events, the organization's inability to notify customers was identified by customers as being non-transparent resulting in a loss of revenue or having to give credit to customers to maintain the relationship. One of the worst occurrences could be finding child pornography on the organization's computer system causing required reporting to law enforcement, loss of employees, and system components that hold company critical data.

- Organizational issues: These issues could include mismanagement, and changes in managerial practices that cause customers to rethink the environment and purchase of products. Like the reputational issues listed above, it is easy to find events where an organization's loyalty, mission statement, or ethics are questioned and harmed, as they are pinned to a mistake, fraudulent act, misconstrued marketing campaigns, or other conduct that places the organization in the media's focus or even a social media frenzy.

- Natural events: Events such as severe weather, earthquakes, or similar disturbances have geographical effects that encumber the resources that your organization may normally lean on for its resiliency. A power outage due to a transformer on your organization's property is localized as a replacement may be near hand. But a natural occurrence that blankets the environment with snow, ice, rockslides, earth subsidence, liquefaction, or high winds, may require the organizations you have relationships with to prioritize life-saving organizations with their products. Your organization may fall low on the scale for getting serviced or obtaining part replacements. If the crisis is a disaster on a very large scale, the transportation of everything essential will be delayed to a point of months without the ability to move products or provide services to your organization's customers.

- Confrontational crisis: Events such as a boycott, strike, protest, or the inability of your workforce to enter the facility, all demand workarounds, negotiation skills, and legal teams working toward a solution to resolve or negate the confrontational event harming your organization.
- Malicious actions: Smear campaigns, character assassinations, or discrediting the statements of your organization can all be harmful and can be a crisis that removes your organization from its function. Public relations and being able to lean on relationships developed through networking and extended loyalty can prevent the damage from such events.
- Human-made crisis: All events that are identified as being caused by mistake or malice can be rolled into this category. Whether a cyber-attack was directed to best your organizational structure, or an employee clicked on a malicious link, the cascading effects on the organization are similar. Consider other issues, such as releasing critical company private data in an email to customers, or an employee with inappropriate ties to a hard right or left group releasing the home addresses of your employees. The potential damage can be horrifying.
- Crisis of violence: And of course, in today's world, we cannot forget about the potential of violence, whether that be an active shooter, a domestic dispute between employees, or a person having a psychotic episode within your facility.
- Combination crisis: You may have noticed that regardless of the category, most are combination-forming. The initial cause is only that, the follow-on crisis is caused by the actions or inactions from that point forward. Preparing, planning, and training for just one crisis is not advised. What may be best is to plan for an all-hazard event, with specifics to select events that affect your organization.

Based on how catastrophic the event was and the breadth and depth of the term crisis, courseware could easily be separated into individual responsibilities, supervisor responsibilities, and managerial actions. A crisis can affect the entire organization, so the course could be larger, or maybe the course you are developing only deals with the security operations or security's response to a crisis. Regardless, coordination with other departments and organizational management may be necessary.

Train the Plan

The primary focus of this training should be the crisis plan developed for the entire organization. The plan should have been developed to identify the risks associated with your organization, the environment, its personnel, and specific locations. The primary purpose of the plan is to increase resiliency through hardening vulnerabilities that have been assessed during the planning process.

Each staff member does not need to be trained on the entire plan but does require training on an overview of the plan, its purpose, and the critical requirements of your organization's need to be resilient during any crisis. After the overview, separate your staff by their roles in the plan and during any crisis. The roles can be by department, managerial roles, or simply manpower.

For example, during a crisis, the physical security team will have a large role in dealing with almost all crisis events. The primary role will be to continue maintaining a high level of security for the organization and personnel while assisting in expediting the movement of equipment, contract staff, or employees. If the crisis is an assault on the facility, security will be dealing with the event by limiting access to everyone except responding authorities. Communication is critical in such events, specifically to responding personnel.

An important part of crisis management is knowing limitations. During the training, educate other departments on the limitations of your staff, what critical tasks they will be performing during such an event, and what tasks they will not be available to perform. An example is if security is unavailable to handle normal access control, other staff will need to recognize the issue and minimize movement for the duration of the event.

Training for managerial roles is critical to the successful mitigation and resumption of services. Supervisors and managers who have specific tasks should already be a part of the plan and identified as critical resources. Managerial personnel not directly affected by a crisis should know their role in maintaining their department's level of performance and lessen the load placed on departments directly affected by the event. Most important will be to maintain communications and reporting when data is requested.

Define the Need

Your organization's crisis plan will identify the need for training, its depth and breadth by department, staff levels, and specific training objectives for key personnel. Generalized training of staff may be available through video or email. However, more specific training should be geared toward supervisory personnel in how to handle such an event, how to assist in the planning, what is expected of security, and the continued security of the facility and its personnel. The criticality of rapid access by responding personnel or authorities should be planned for and exceptions to some rules should be justified and accepted by alternative processes.

Staff members providing the training should be experienced with the plan, crisis management, and how your organization will minimize vulnerabilities through redundancies and any additional contingencies that may need to be prepared.

If this training is required by a standard to which your organization subscribes, ensure the training needs complete all the requirements for that standard. If subscribing to multiple standards requires similar training in this area, analyze to ensure all items of the standards are covered.

Conduct a Task Analysis

Your organization has put forth a considerable effort to research and document the many risks involved with the vulnerabilities that could lead to a crisis. It is therefore recommended that your task analysis not only conform to the standards but consider the job at hand for your department personnel during such an emergency. Your experiences and those of your organization are a good place to start. You can also talk to your peers who have had such an occurrence to see what stumbling blocks their staff had to overcome during a crisis that required additional emphasis on topics during the training.

Of critical importance, every crisis or disaster needs to have a post-event briefing and an analysis of what worked, what did not, and what additions or deletions of roles or processes are recommended. What needs refreshing, and what contracts need to be renegotiated or reconsidered in total? There are always better ways to handle bad days, your job is to train your staff so that they assist in the event and not cause a hindrance to reclamation, slowing respondents to the site where they are needed, or failing to communicate due to inability or unpreparedness for disaster situations.

If you have had a recent event, list the event and anything that could have been done better. Think outside the box and recognize what alike events could be handled similarly.

Here are a handful of items that your training may want to cover:

- Parking and traffic flow, and barriers. This is opening the access portals for vehicles but not allowing the vehicle to park in a manner that reduces access to future necessary vehicles. Are barriers needed to deploy to keep vehicles out of danger zones, where are they kept when not in use, and how will they be moved to where needed?
- Facility access and badging, visitor badging, or just a brief identity check. Firefighters are not going to stop for you to collect their identification. However, it would be a good bet that the responders in official uniforms or turn-out gear have been identified before your event by their departments. Their names should be sufficient for access records.
- Use of closed areas, and emergency egress doors. During an evacuation, alarmed exit doors will be used, potentially causing calls for security services or alarms in the command center.
- During emergencies, access to the facility through egress-only doors may be necessary. Having an access method such as a "Knox® Box" or similar near those doors is important to assist with emergency response access while still maintaining control.
- If your site is still so secure that emergency respondents need to be escorted by security, what is the locus of controls for escorting personnel and do the escorts have the ability to access all the doors in the facility? If access control is throughout your facility, a go-bag for emergency responders is common with maps, identifiers, radios, and access badges.
- Additional office arrangements, computer equipment, and network access. Should an event such as a leak or building damage cause employees to be relocated, a designated site, available rooms, desks, chairs, computers, network access, and other needs will be stressed.
- Potential red-team access. If the event is cyber, a red-team responding team will need network and computer access beyond most employees. Such a team will require a prior authorized contract with a company that can respond quickly with ample personnel to handle the event.
- Reasonable safety efforts. During a disaster or crisis, safety should still be a strong consideration as additional employees being hurt by falling debris, or slipping on a wet carpet will

cause the organization to lose more personnel capabilities and requires others to be taken from their post to care for the now injured.

- Depending on the event and the size of the impact on your organization, halting all removal of information from network devices may be a consideration. There is always a potential for a physical attack or event to be masking a potentially larger cyber security event.
- Events should be documented and the only way to do that is from the initiation of the event. Have a dedicated person in the command structure acting as a scribe that keeps a running log identifying when things were known, names of personnel, who made critical decisions, and more. The log can later be used to assist in documenting the event for evaluation of effort, analysis of the occurrence, and future planning. There is an increasing need to provide a copy of the after-action report to internal and external clients, as the depth of the report gives clues as to process-driven adherence.
- Threat assessment may also take a sidestep during a disaster but security should have an eye on every person who enters the site of the event. There are numerous recordings of unknown people showing up during an event just to walk around and see what is happening. If they have been in your facility, they will be walking out with more information than they came in with.
- Even during the smallest event, there is a potential that employees will require physical and mental care.
- Should the event's duration require staff to be on-site for a prolonged period, what prepositioned materials and housing are available for those individuals?
- Who is the site commander in control? When a crisis is identified who is placed in immediate control? When a more senior person arrives can that person take over as site commander? Seniority and title are not inherently necessary to be a site commander during a crisis. The CEO or other senior executives should be handling other critical initiatives during the event and not be in command of the crisis. Similarly, the site commander is not suggested to be a person who is doing the labor, as this takes away from command oversight. Your security team needs to know who the site commander is as taking direction from multiple people is usually counterproductive.

- Who can call the event a crisis and initiate the crisis plan? This may seem like an administrative item, but initiating the crisis plan has requirements, so using the plan for small events is not recommended, though training and planning for large events will give strength and capabilities to your staff for smaller non-crisis events.
- Calling personnel to the site has a cost. Therefore, the person who calls in personnel before their shift, or during their day off has a great responsibility and should be identified in the plan, and more importantly to your department supervisors.
- If the event is of considerable size and duration, or your organization has a production line that uses several workers, that personnel may be able to assist in dealing with the event. So, who can put production on hold to utilize personnel in other duties? Similar to calling in personnel on their off-time, putting a company on a production hold has greater down-the-road effects.
- Should your organization have preplanned and negotiated contracts to assist in a crisis, who can make the call to initiate that relationship, and who are the points of contact at those companies? If no contract exists, who in your organization can call and pay to have materials delivered?

Develop the Objectives

At the organizational level, the plan needs to be introduced to all staff members involved in participating with the plan requiring that course objectives be developed for all aspects of the crisis plan's training efforts.

Anyone involved with crisis management must know that the plan exists, where the information is kept, who is responsible for the plan, and most importantly what are the employees' duties and responsibilities. Just acknowledging that there is a plan with general information conveyed in an email, company newsletter, or in conjunction with a safety meeting, daily briefing, or other employee meetings may be enough for most staff. This does not preclude the need for a course objective nor does it preclude the need for record-keeping of who is in attendance.

Example:

With the increased regularity of "active shooter" incidents, organizations should have some training for their employees should an event occur. Several years ago, the US Department of Homeland Security came up with the "Run,

Hide, Fight" protocol. Granted not the perfect training to survive an active shooter, however, what is the perfect training for this?

The "Run, Hide, Fight" training is simple, easy to remember, a catchy name, and most importantly it gives the employees direction that they are responsible for their survival. After being in security for too many years, I recognize that trying to tell others what to do in a frightening event has about a 50% success rate. And the security of your organization can be held responsible should the directions given cause harm to the group.

A primary benefit to the security department of the Run, Hide, Fight training is that security will be very busy with the direct incident and not be available to give direction to the other employees. Security will not be able to answer phone calls, texts, or emails asking for updates or information. If your department is advanced in weapons use to pursue the shooter, or acting as a conduit for responding agencies, Run, Hide, Fight takes the extra responsibility away from your department and allows your people to do their jobs.

Any group of employees with specific responsibilities, such as security, cyber-security, network technicians, critical infrastructure maintenance, and all managerial positions, should have specific training for the plan. Therefore, each group may require a complete curriculum and objectives.

When developing the objectives for this training, an overall course objective should give broad strokes as to the purpose of the plan and the intended responsibilities of all employees to assist in putting the plan into action.

Departments or groups of employees with specific tasks in the plan should have individual course objectives and then detailed terminal objectives covering tasks. The number of your enabling objectives will depend on the grouping of the above tasks and how in-depth your department is involved in the event planning and coordination.

Based on your task analysis and organizational approval, develop the topics in a smooth flow and develop objectives accordingly so that objectives overlap and build toward a conclusion of skills and knowledge.

Lastly, how will the objectives be tested to ensure the students have reached comprehension and the ability to put the new knowledge to use? In this case, testing and even practice may not be necessary so ensuring comprehension may require continued reminder communications.

Define the Training Form

Focusing only on the training of the security department, the curriculum will probably be initiated through short notices that can be sent via email or delivered at a shift briefing. The skillsets required for the security department during crises should be common to your staff's capabilities. It is, however, the aggregate crisis mode that will require quick situational assessment and decisions based on the evolving situation and needs of the organization.

Using the active shooter situation as a worse-case situation, your staff's willingness to engage the shooter, approach, weapons use, marksmanship, tactical team movement, room clearing, unified command, combat first aid, and communication must be discussed well before such an event.

Write the Curriculum

The curriculum documentation allows for consistency in the training and especially the staff's readiness should a crisis occur. As the plan will continue to evolve with relationships with vendors and new technologies and processes, the curriculum should be written to accept changes without much shuffling of courseware. Each of those responsible for oversight of a crisis should be able to understand and comprehend the course objectives and put the new knowledge to use.

Draft the courseware to recognize the responsibilities, and abilities of your staff, and to ensure the objective of assignments is satisfactory to the criteria you have set.

Develop Testing

This course could be considered introductory to the main body of the organization and advanced training for specialized personnel, and supervisory and managerial members. Those conducting this training should be able to communicate well, tackle tough discussions, and maintain flexibility while being able to make quick decisions based on knowledge of the organizational standards. Therefore, the testing of those in this training may be multi-faceted or simply conduct a tabletop exercise and have supervision assist.

11

Training for Security Managers and Directors

INTRODUCTION

The knowledge and experience required to be a manager or director of security services have a few basic requirements but too often are widely varied for all the right reasons. Organizational needs are probably the primary driver behind the definition. Each organization looking to hire a security manager is typically looking for the same core knowledge that fits its needs. The needs of a contract security company may be different from those of a pharmaceutical manufacturer or a hospital, a data center, a non-profit, or a corporate high-rise in downtown Mumbai or New York.

For these reasons, the candidate you are training for security management needs to fit your requirements. If you are the Security Director or Chief Security Officer (CSO), you need a candidate who either already has the characteristics that you need or you must be willing to provide the education and training for your required skill sets.

As was written in the prior section on Security Supervisor Training, terms such as supervisor, supervision, manager, management, leader, and leadership are too often interchangeable. Finding training that fits the individual roles is tough as companies would rather hire someone with proven experience and assume they already have the necessary knowledge.

DOI: 10.4324/9781003292586-14

In this text, the term manager/director will include security practitioners in all manners of security that have the responsibility to oversee the judicious treatment of security staff including employee evaluation, guidance, conducting shift briefings, giving shift assignments, ensuring posts are relived for breaks and lunches as needed, ensure reports and documents are correct before they are passed to management, and confirm the conduct of the shift is performing to standards.

So, what are managers? Managers are responsible for the selection criteria for new staff, promotions, pay increases, hiring/firing personnel, budgets, strategic planning, systems design, enterprise risk, architectural security implementation and design, interfacing directly regarding planned Human Resources events, policy/procedure/practice development, legal, or operational department plans, or networking with law enforcement and government agencies.

The field of expertise for the security manager may increase their responsibilities as with cyber, loss prevention, physical, intelligence, threat assessment, incident resolution and notification, assisting sales in acquiring new clients, policy enforcement, systems installation, or design. Combine these functions with the fact that management is the process of organizing, controlling, and administrating an effort. In your organization, mixing selected security disciplines with your functional needs can be anything from finances, logistics, personnel, and services.

So, where do you start in identifying what skills you need to train, and what skills can you accept from experience in a candidate?

Within your organization, I assume you want a manager who can lead others, oversee a portion or all of your security operations including planning, budgeting, dealing with personnel issues, conducting threat assessment on facilities under their control, developing security system plans, developing requests for proposal and negotiate contracts with contract security companies and systems providers, understand legal issues regarding background investigations, questioning position candidates, coaching subordinates toward the next level, and produce reports required by your industry and organization.

One trait of a good managerial candidate is a myopic view of events. How wide is your candidate's knowledge, experience, and view of an incident, its aftermath, and maybe the need for a process? Keeping that in

/

mind, these are the tasks that every security managerial candidate should have knowledge and experience. What is missing is the ability to take in information and consider the positives and consequences of responding to events following organizational standards and company and regional norms. This trait is commonly called critical thinking and is not easily trained. However, this is critically important if the experience or knowledge does not fit the organization.

A college or university degree in a variety of disciplines will provide a basis for your candidate's knowledge. Many schools offer degrees in Homeland Security, Criminal Justice, Strategic Security, and other courses aimed toward issues of national security. These are excellent as the person paying for and taking the coursework will remain engaged during the classes and in the performance of exercises and writing. However, these are not the only degrees that will make a great security manager.

SECURITY INDUSTRY STANDARDS

In the recent 2023, "Security Officers and Patrol Services Competency Model" developed by the International Foundation for Protection Officers (IFPO) for the United States Department of Labor, near the bottom of the pyramid is the Academic Competencies. These same academic competencies were also included in the 1993 University of Phoenix and ASIS Foundation report "Enterprise Security Risks and Workforce Competencies – Findings From an Industry Roundtable on Security Talent Development" and in the 2020 United States Department of Labor "Enterprise Security Competency Model."

Understandably these are not solely collegiate requirements, they are simply competencies that are required for higher development. They include:

- *Security Fundamentals* – Understand and apply basic security principles to the security of the enterprise or a specific structure, system, or process.
- *Business Foundations* – Understand basic business principles, trends, and economics.
- *Critical and Analytical Thinking* – Using logic, reasoning, and analysis to address problems.

- *Communications* – Giving full attention to what others are saying and communicating in English well enough to be understood by others.
- *Reading and Writing* – Understanding written sentences and paragraphs in work-related documents. Using standard English to compile information and prepare written reports.
- *STEM (Science, Technology, Engineering, and Mathematics) Literacy* – Understand and apply science, technology, engineering, and mathematics to work within individual roles and responsibilities and in collaborating with allied workers.

The topics identified in these reports should provide a starting point for your management training. However, if you are looking for the pinnacle of security management training requirements, the ASIS International CSO Center, in a May 2023 Security Management article, states the following five areas of competence are required for a CSO to be successful.

Listed in a pyramid the five areas of competence are:

Future Proofing
Analyze and improve your organization's roadmap, leverage the latest technologies, and ensure physical security remains pro-active, not reactive.

Strategy
Devise long-term strategic goals that close identified gaps, improve readiness, and better anticipate and integrate with the goals of the business.

Risk Management
Build a program that can assess risk, identify gaps, and combine data with expertise to translate security requirements into the language of business.

Analyzing the Business
Evaluate your security program and its place in the wider business; identify strong competencies and relationships, as well as areas of growth.

Leadership and Management
Develop soft skills including people management and develop-ment programs and project leadership; nurture lasting relation-ships with business partners; implement change management and create impactful communications.

The simplest review of these requirements shows a vast chasm of requirements with little substance for your organizational-specific training curriculum. There is a valid reason for the gap – it is up to your organizational needs and your industry sector to determine what subjects to train.

One standard that you may want to review is the International Foundation of Security Officers (IFPO), Certified in Security Supervision and Management (CSSM). The course curriculum shows IFPO's depth of knowledge necessary for a security officer to rise through the ranks of the profession.

Topics included in the courseware:

Future of private security	Security personnel selection
Motivation and evaluation	Security officer scheduling
Interpersonal communications	Staff training and development
Company policies and procedures	Testimony in court
Managing/supervising to reduce liability	Risk and crisis management
Statistical analysis	Investigations
Legal aspects of security	Sexual harassment
Security medical response	Designing operations centers
Security technologies	Workplace violence
Crime prevention/community relations	Supervisor's role in training
Testing for learning retention	

ASIS International has both the Associate Protection Professional (APP) and the Certified Protection Professional (CPP). The APP knowledge base is a portion of the CPP knowledge base, and the requirements for experience in security supervision are lesser.

Both the APP and CPP bodies of knowledge are taken from the *Protection of Assets Manual* published by ASIS International and five additional standards, two of which are ANSI Standards and are also published by ASIS International. The CPP requires knowledge of seven industry standards published by ASIS International.

The APP is touted by ASIS as the "first 'rung' of a security manager's career ladder." The requirement for security management experience is one to four years or a combination of security management experience and college degrees.

The curriculum consists of four domains:

Security Fundamentals	Business Operations
Risk Management	Response Management

The ASIS International CPP Standard has been considered the pinnacle of security management certification for as long as I can remember. It is globally recognized and has great value in our industry.

Eligibility for this certification requires nine years in security and at least three years have been "responsible charge of a security function."

The curriculum consists of seven heavily researched domains with a depth that requires the candidates to show an understanding of the concepts more than simply answering questions.

Security principles and practices:

- Business principles and practices
- Investigations
- Personnel security
- Physical security
- Information security
- Crisis management

On the information security side of our industry, the SANS Institute has courseware on "Security Leadership Essentials for Managers." The course is geared toward newly appointed security managers, information security officers, aspiring certified information security officers, and other security professionals.

The program covers five domains that include:

- Governance to plan a security program.
- Architecture to design security capabilities.
- Engineering to build security capabilities.
- Build and lead the team, process, and culture.
- Run operations to manage and mitigate attacks.

SANS touts the skills learned from attending the class to be:

- Make sense of different cybersecurity frameworks.
- Understand and analyze risk.
- Understand the pros and cons of different reporting relationships.

- Manage and lead technical teams and projects.
- Build a vulnerability management program.
- Inject security into modern software development workflows.
- Strategically leverage a security incident and event management (SIEM).
- Lead a Security Operations Center (SOC).
- Change behavior and build a security-aware culture.
- Effectively manage security projects.
- Enable modern security architectures and the cloud.
- Build security engineering capabilities using automation and infrastructure as code.
- Get up to speed quickly on information security issues and terminology.
- Establish a minimum standard of security knowledge, skills, and abilities.
- Speak the same language as technical security professionals.

The International Association of Healthcare Security and Safety (IAHSS) also has a certification for Certified Healthcare Protection Administrators (CHPA). Their certification is geared toward management levels and above, security professionals. Their Certified Healthcare Security Supervisor covers a range of topics including:

- Establishing Policies, Processes, and Procedures
  - Review Security Management Plans and Performance Improvement Plans
- Selecting and Managing Employees
  - Hiring, Onboarding, and Scheduling Employees
  - Managing and Retaining Employees
  - Evaluations, Progressive Discipline, and Termination
- Developing and Managing Officer Training Programs
  - Analyzing Training Needs, Developing and Designing an Effective Program and Materials
  - Implementing and Evaluating Training
- Mitigating Risks and Managing Incidents
  - Root Cause Analysis (RCA)
- Reviewing Reports and Making Informed Decisions
  - Analyzing Data and Making Informed Decisions

With these well-researched standards, conducted by associations and foundations for and of our industry, some developed with like-minded associations, there is a double benefit of providing time and money for your staff to attain these certifications and others that these organizations offer. If your research and task analysis find a majority of the key points of their curriculum fit your organizational needs, then there may be no need to rethink the wheel. Secondly, your organization benefits from your staff holding industry-accepted certifications in their profession, bolstering the collective knowledge of your staff. Thirdly, should your processes ever be questioned in a court of law, being able to point to the research conducted by a notable organization, the training, and testing being conducted by the same and the vast number of other certified professionals in the world would indicate that the training you provided your staff is the same as the entire industry provides (Figure 11.1).

	1	2	3	4	5	6	7	8	9	Needs	Priority
Leadership				X							
Security Fundamentals	X	X	X			X	X				
- Apply Basic Security Principles	X	X	X			X	X				
Business Foundations	X	X	X			X					
- Understand basic business principles	X	X	X			X					
- Business trends	X	X	X	X		X					
- Business Economics	X	X	X			X					
Critical and Analytical Thinking	X	X	X								
- Logic	X	X	X								
- reasoning	X	X	X								
- analyze	X	X	X								
Communications	X	X	X		X						
- Listening	X	X	X		X						
Reading	X	X	X								
- Understand written sentences and paragraphs	X	X	X								
Writing	X	X	X								
- Compile information and prepare reports	X	X	X								
STEM Literacy	X	X	X								
- Apply STEM in security roles	X	X	X	X				X			
- Apply STEM in collaborating with others	X	X	X	X				X			

(Left margin label: SUPERVISOR)

Figure 11.1 Supervisor/manager topic matrix.

Note: The left side of the table is labeled vertically "MANAGER / DIRECTOR".

Future Proofing			X				X	
- Leverage the latest technology			X			X		
- Proactive physical security			X	X	X			
Strategy			X	X		X	X	
- Long-term goals that close gaps			X			X	X	
- Improve readiness			X			X	X	
- Anticipate and integrate with business goals			X			X	X	
Risk Management			X	X	X	X		
- Build a Program to Assess Risk			X	X		X		
- Build a Program to identify risk gaps			X	X		X	X	
- Combine data with security expertise			X	X		X	X	
- Translate security requirements into business language			X					
Analyze Business			X				X	
- Evaluate security programs for its place in business			X	X		X	X	
- Identify strong competencies and relationships			X					
- Identify areas of growth			X				X	
Leadership & Management			X			X	X	
- Develop soft skills			X	X				
- People management			X	X		x	X	
- People Development Program			X	X		X	X	
- Project Leadership			X			X		
- Nurture Business Partner relationships			X					
- Implement Change Management			X			X		
- Create Impactful Communications			X					
Future of Private Security				X				
Security Personnel Selection				X	X		X	
Motivation and Evaluation				X		X	X	
Security Officer Scheduling				X			X	
Interpersonal Communications				X				
Staff Training and Development				X		X	X	

Figure 11.1   (*continued*)

Company Policies and Procedures				X			X	X	
Court Testimony				X					
Managing / Supervising to reduce liability				X			X	X	
Risk and Crisis Management				X	X	X		X	
Statistical Analysis				X				X	
Investigations				X		X			
Legal Aspects of Security				X			X		
Sexual Harassment				X					
Security Medical Response				X					
Designing Operations Centers				X		X	X		
Security Technologies				X		X	X		
Workplace Violence				X					
Crime Prevention/Community Relations				X					
Supervisor's Role in Training				X			X	X	
Testing for Learning Retention				X				X	
Security Fundamentals					X	X			
Business Operations					X		X	X	
Risk Management					X			X	
Response Management					X			X	
Security Principles and Practices						X		X	
Investigations						X			
Personnel Security						X			
Physical Security						X			
Information Security						X			
Crisis Management						X		X	
Governance to plan a security program							X		
Cyber Architecture to Design Security Capabilities							X		
Cyber Engineering to build security capabilities							X		
Build and lead the team, process, and culture							X	X	
Establish Policies, Processes, and Procedures								X	
- Review Security Plans								X	
- Develop Performance Improvement Plans								X	

Figure 11.1 *(continued)*

Selecting and Managing Employees									X		
- Hiring, Onboarding, and Scheduling Employees									X		
- Managing and Retaining Employees									X		
- Evaluations, Progressive Discipline, and Termination									X		
Developing and Managing Officer Training Program									X		
- Analyze Training Needs, Develop and Design an Effective Program and Materials									X		
- Implement and Evaluating Training									X		
Mitigating Risk and Managing Incidents									X		
- Root Cause Analysis									X		
Reviewing Reports and Making Informed Decisions									X		
- Analyzing Data and Making Informed Decisions									X		

Key to Source of Information in the Above Matrix:

1 2023 "Security Officers and Patrol Services Competency Model" developed by the IFPO for the United States Department of Labor

2 2020 United States Department of Labor "Enterprise Security Competency Model"

3 1993 University of Phoenix and ASIS Foundation report "Enterprise Security Risks and Workforce Competencies

4 ASIS International CSO Center, in a May 2023 Security Management

5 IFPO Certified in Security Supervision and Management (CSSM)

6 ASIS International, Associate Protection Professional

7 ASIS International, Certified Protection Professional

8 SANS Security Leadership Essentials for Managers

9 IAHSS Certified Healthcare Protection Administrator (CHPA)

Figure 11.1 (*continued*)

ORGANIZATIONAL REQUIREMENTS

We are all in the same profession and some with special functions, but the greatest difference is your organization and how it operates. With the differences, what are the training needs of your organization for managerial personnel? And what are the managerial talents you need to grow within your department? Are they geared more toward business, budgeting, intelligence collection and modeling for reporting, crime prevention through environmental design (CPTED), security systems design, surveillance camera coverage, video recording specification writing, or maybe risk and site assessments for executive protection?

Your department may need all of the topics listed above, if so, then prioritizing the needs for curriculum development, budgeting, candidate selection and time will become the next issue to tackle. To assist in identifying and prioritizing the topical needs, using the standards listed above, a gap analysis in spreadsheet form might help.

BUDGETING AND FINANCIAL

Financials are the basis of any organization as it takes funds to run an operation. Regardless if your organization is a non-profit, for-profit commercial company, or a government organization, the cost of doing business needs to be budgeted, funded, and the use of the expended funds accounted for. In a common operating security department, the most critical aspects of financials are the budgeting process, reviewing the fund flow, and letting finance know when you will need funds for large purchases.

Budgeting is normally on a calendar year or fiscal year basis. Whether the budget starts in January and goes to the end of December or starts within the year, such as November, and goes through the end of October, the importance of the budgeting process is matching your spending needs to your calendar.

Budgets are intended so that there is a plan for spending funds throughout the calendar period, allowing for finance to only make funds available as needed for that month. No budget is perfect but keeping the finance department apprised of your spending needs is critical to the organization. Budgets are monitored and altered as needed.

Define the Need

Budgeting is critical to your department's operational health and it creates an efficient method of spending funds for only critical needs or needs that are anticipated throughout the year. Your budget process should be able to sit on top of your annual operation schedule, with fund allocations occurring just before the purchase or spending.

If your organization is a security contracting company, the budget may also include the need to bring income to the business so that the operation continues.

Few have had experience in the budget process and most have had to guess their way through or follow in another's footsteps. Providing a course to train your staff in budgeting should be considered a forward leap in organizational development. Exercising your network within the organization by engaging a finance department peer can save the entire organization in preparing and auditing budgets.

The more geographically diverse your department operates, the more your team needs to be trained. There is a need for your management team to be educated in the budgeting process and how the organizational financials are critical to the operation.

Conduct a Task Analysis

If you are not formally trained in the budget process or organizational financials, ask your finance department to help you put together a task list for a proposed training on the subject.

Responsibilities

- What are the functions within the finance department?
- Who sets financial policies?
- Who is responsible for the budget, its approval, and adjustments?
- Setting spending goals
- Avoid disallowed spending
- Spend funds effectively
- Audit Function
- Types of budgets
- Organizational Budget – complete budget for the entire organization to include budgets for Programs, Divisions, Sections, Capital, Cash-flow, Opportunities

Determine Training Form

An assumption may be that most of this course can be done through lectures, whether in-person or computer-based. However, as budgeting is a skill, an additional exercise in making a budget might be helpful to put the concepts of finances together. Using real-life dollar amounts and future spending for your department will have a great benefit to the time spent in training.

Based on the task analysis and in communication with the finance department, determine how long you propose the course will take in hours.

As this subject is of a higher academic level, you may consider finding a collegiate course in the area that your staff can attend to gain this training. However, organizational organic knowledge will not be put forth in a college course.

Develop Objectives

Based on the task analysis and maybe a little assistance from the finance department, develop a course objective and then terminal objectives to cover the knowledge your organization needs your staff to know.

If it is determined that a skill should be included in the course, identify the specifics of the skill. If the overall skill is to develop a sample project budget for purchasing and installing water rail barriers around critical infrastructure, the associated objectives might be:

- Identify three suitable products from three vendors and obtain per unit and multiple unit purchase costs to include shipping and lead time for delivery, using organizational-friendly vendors before other vendors.
- With the products, determine the number of items required.
- Using the provided format, develop a budget spreadsheet and written report for the project purchase and deployment.

Write the Curriculum

Budgeting and finance policies and procedures are often changed in organizations to follow current practices of the industry, or the financial sector based on audit criteria, however, a broad spectrum course covering the processes of finance and budgets along with a skills exercise should well equip your staff with the knowledge and skills necessary to assist in the department's budgets. As the budget and project processes are ongoing, the curriculum should be written so the student understands why some projects or budget line items go unfunded. Management personnel in your department should be able to understand and comprehend the course objectives and put the new knowledge to use.

Draft the courseware to recognize the responsibilities, and abilities of your staff, and to ensure the objective of assignments is satisfactory to the criteria you have set.

Develop Testing

This course could be considered advanced training for specialized personnel, and supervisory and managerial members. Those conducting this training should be able to communicate well, tackle tough discussions, and maintain flexibility while being able to discuss the organizational standards. Therefore, the testing of those in this training may be multi-faceted or simply conduct a tabletop exercise and have supervision to assist.

NOTE:
I assumed the students in this course are well versed in the standardized software used by your organization. If not, a course on the software may be required before the exercise portion of this course.

MENTORING

Many of us have started projects or increased our areas of responsibility with little knowledge of where to begin, how to deal with certain issues, or what are the next steps. Having a mentor or someone to whom you can call and ask broad-based questions about how they completed a similar task, or how they think you should proceed can be comforting as well as allow your management to have confidence in your ability to complete the task.

Being a mentor is not always easy as we learned a great deal from our parents, former supervisors, drill instructors, training officers, or watch commanders, and not all of what we learned was beneficial in all situations though they tried to fit the problem and solution into their style of leadership. You need to be cautious about following their lead in this manner. I called similar situations "Dad-isms." The good "Dad-isms" were: "stand when someone speaks with you," and "be the first to say hello or shake hands." But the bad "Dad-isms" were being disappointed, or mad when a subordinate makes a bad decision. If you fired everyone when they made a mistake you would be the only person at the job.

Making a mistake is part of development, it is your job to train the staff well enough that the mistakes are small and correctable, and if needed retraining should be the harshest remedy.

Herein lies a big problem with mentoring your staff, when they come asking you a question, they want to know how you would do it and then they will follow suit. It may be expeditious but not growth-inducing. In the "Dad-ism" world, when confronted with such a question from a subordinate, you will probably want to fix their issue for them. In mentoring this is the wrong approach. In a mentor-mentee relationship, your job is to listen to their problem, ask questions regarding a solution, and then steer them in the generally correct direction. Unless they are far from a road map for success.

Mentorship is not as much a course but a set of guidelines to be followed by anyone appointed to be a mentor. The course should give a new mentor the rule sets, and guidance to avoid the pitfalls of bad "Dad-isms."

Define the Need

The greatest need here is to minimize the time your subordinates take making the same mistakes you may have made. Allowing mistakes is a great learning environment but minimizing the size and repercussions of those mistakes is the hopeful goal of coaching or mentoring.

The size of your department will also have a great deal of impact regarding setting up a coaching or mentorship program. The more subordinate managers and supervisors the greater the benefit of this effort.

If embarking on this endeavor, have a short course in teaching others how to be a coach or mentor. Remember to include topics such as:

- Active listening
- Form a contract to ensure the relationship stays within bounds
- Identify reportable events
- Measure a period for meetings and the length of the relationship.

Conduct a Task Analysis

Similar to all curricula and keeping within your standards of curriculum administration and form, a task analysis will need to be performed to ensure the correct amount of time and thought has been put into this effort. All efforts take time and resources, since one intent of coaching and mentoring is to minimize the time of errors, the evolution of this relationship needs documentation and development.

Conducting interviews with your managers and supervisors to identify how such relationships would benefit the department, as well as a listing of past issues that could have been mitigated through a conversation with a mentor, are the first steps to the analysis.

Venturing outside of your department to peers and other organizational departments can also have a welcoming effect. Consider the greater benefits of being inclusive to your organization by offering this course to other departments for their use. Depending on the managerial level of your senior staff, being mentored by a senior executive in another department can have a very valuable outcome.

Determine Training Form

The initial or introductory course on how to be a coach or mentor may easily fit into a discussion being led by an instructor, or in a lecture format.

A separate or inclusive course for those to be coached should also be developed as this is an atypical form of training with no set outcomes yet with form and function in a business manner. Setting and maintaining a business-style relationship is necessary so that neither the coach nor those to be coached are not wasting time and are benefitting from the exercise.

After the introductory lesson, a recommendation is for the coach and candidate to pair up based on several criteria that the organization deems necessary. Availability undoubtedly will be a critical requirement and therefore setting time parameters is important to avoid wasting time. Though the time and duration of the engagement are up to the pace and evolution of your department, a recommendation would be that the candidate meets with the coach weekly at a convenient yet scheduled time to discuss the past week's events and upcoming issues. Also, setting a contracted period is important as the relationship will last for one calendar year. Setting the expectation that this relationship will be a year-long gives merit to the exercise and allows time for the relationship to mature.

The hope will be that the relationship will continue after the course period and train both the coach and candidate in how to discuss issues and what options are available as solutions.

Develop Objectives

Objectives developed based on the task analysis are still the format to be used. The course objective covers the intent of the course while motivating the use of coaching. Topic objects may not require ensuring an understanding or testing, but items determined to be necessary from the task analysis should be listed as objectives.

Write the Curriculum

The course itself may be quick in that the lecture or discussion may only take an instructor an hour to cover the objectives and materials. Keeping the organizational curriculum format of a Lesson Topic Guide is still valuable in this case, thereby keeping all curricula in a standardized form.

Develop Testing

This course could be considered advanced training for specialized personnel, and supervisory and managerial members. And though a formal test may not be developed for this course, a metric needs to be established to ensure the time and effort of candidates and coaches are not wasted. Developing a simple formatted meeting journal for the coach to complete at every meeting, allowing the candidate to have a comment space for lessons learned or issued side-stepped by the conversation is critical to formalizing the course.

EXECUTIVE PROTECTION

Regardless of the form of security your department provides, there may be the need to protect an executive or key personnel who are visiting your facilities. VIP Security, dignitary detail, or executive protection, regardless of the moniker placed on the practice, are all a form of specialized security unlike that which the daily security efforts are used to performing, therefore, have a plan as to how your team will offer such a service, how they are deployed, the gathering of threat data, and an overview of personal protection.

Well before it is necessary, have a plan and discuss the expectations of your team and what they should be prepared for while providing this form of security.

There are plenty of examples of poor personal protection details that place the protected at greater risk through mistakes and security not understanding their responsibilities.

- The US Presidential limousine getting high centered on a driveway exit, requiring special tow trucks to assist in getting the vehicle free without damage and necessitating the protectee to be moved to another vehicle.
- Security detail watching a performance by the protectee instead of scanning for threats.
- The subject being protected exiting a store first with the security agent following with arms full of packages, unable to react to protect.
- One of the biggest mistakes was the executive surviving an assassination attempt, disregarding the threat, and continuing un-protected where he was killed soon after by another assassin. It started World War I.

218

In the above mistakes, it is clear that the mistakes were preventable:

- Preplan the route, know the obstacles, and have a plan for mechanical breakdowns, route deviation, or other threats that may occur.
- Train the security detail in what to look for, how to communicate threats, and practice performing the duties.
- A security detail is not a gopher, an extra set of hands, or a friend. Set the expectations of the duties and responsibilities of securing the executive.
- Conduct threat awareness, and threat intelligence, plan the route with security preceding the protectee, plan, and practice evasion techniques, and do not press a threat.

There are a multitude of factors specific to the protection of dignitaries. As the examples above indicate, threat assessment, site selection, pre-event site visits, intelligence gathering, licensing, meeting with local law enforcement, planning the route, selection of vehicles, prepping the vehicles, practicing for the event, meeting with the person to be protected, demonstrating the tactics used for their protection, multi-story building planning, elevator control, and package handling are just a few to consider.

Several professional associations are specific to dignitary protection:

- The Board of Executive Protection Professionals (EP²) has developed an ANSI-accredited standard for dignitary protection. EP2 also has a board certification exam with three knowledge domains:
  - Operational Foundation
  - Operational Progression
  - Operational Management

  For Executive Protection Professionals, training, continuing education on new topics, or refreshing current knowledge is critical. Consider when selecting training events, do not overlook who is delivering the training, what are the training topics and whether the course work is current and relevant. An individual should not just attend training just for the sake of attending training. Also look at training that may be seen as outside the box but makes you more valuable to your current client and to future clients.

  James Cameron, CPP, President/CEO Security Concepts Group LLC, and President/Chairman of the Board of Executive Protection Professionals (EP²)

- ASIS International has a certificate program in Executive Protection. Their Learning Objectives include:
  - Types of executive protection
  - Skills of an executive protection professional
  - The role of threat and vulnerability risk assessments
  - Benefits of protective intelligence
  - Advance activities
- The IFPO has a portion of its Certified Protection Officer and Certified Security Supervisor and Manager Certifications that address dignitary protection.

Candidate selection and an in-depth background investigation including personal interviews with former co-workers and neighbors should be considered as these candidates will have close-quarter contact with the dignitary and will be in earshot of private conversations. These private times are extremely confidential and protection of all aspects of the client information is above all a necessity.

Define the Need

If your organization has dignitaries who need to be protected while on travel, in their homes, or at events, then you need to train staff to conduct executive protection. Determine to what level your team needs to be trained. Like everything else, there are varying degrees of dignitary protection. My experience included executives and their residential security for the families when dignitaries visited one of our facilities, which included two Speakers of the House, several Congressional members, Senators, former Cabinet members, and Presidential candidates. Due to the limited engagement, our tactical training was also limited and included three-person and four-person team movements, shadow movements, and coordination with other security details.

Conduct a Task Analysis

Conducting a task analysis is a great start to assess the needs of your organization, the possible size of a protection team, how specialized they need to be as well as the length and depth of the coursework. If your experience in dignitary protection lacks depth and you have a greater need for more specific training, sending a leading team member to a valid training course may assist in rounding out the training needs assessment as well as assisting in providing your organization with an instructor and practitioner.

Like in other task analysis development, create a list of events that you have had to provide specialized protection and a list of duties, services, and planning conducted for these events. Using this list, adding lessons learned for each event can identify the elementary skills your staff will need to be taught.

A key point to specialized protection events is the fluidity of events, readiness, and flexibility for which your staff must be ready. Know that dignitaries sometimes have different agendas than were passed down to your team.

Some specialized teams require advanced technology, such as a separate command center, scrambled communications, armored vehicles, weapons, and access to threat databases, schedules, and protected networks. But protection of a dignitary may also include the use of CPTED, escape rooms, and other custom and non-typical security devices.

Conducting threat assessments, advance team site visits, and intelligence gathering can easily be separated into its own set of courses. Each has specific tasks that regardless of the reason for the training, can cross over several security needs. Separating these into individual courses will also allow for more time to absorb the material, tactics, and practice.

Determine Training Form

The depth of your courseware will dictate potential multiple training formats. Lecture for general knowledge, discussions, confidentiality, and tabletop exercises for planning and command and control, and field exercises for tactical movement and vehicle operations.

Develop Objectives

Depending on the depth of your training needs, the course might be more manageable if separated into several domains. However, if your coursework is comprised of five separate courses, an all-encompassing course objective that lists the courses within the master course should be developed. It would also be advisable to develop the sub-courses first, then create an umbrella master course objective.

Write the Curriculum

As discussed above, the depth of dignitary protection required by your organization will determine the length and breadth of your course. For an organization that requires a more extreme level of executive protection, this course can be a week-long with multiple add-on lessons for the changes your organization has seen in its protection protocol and practical exercises when downtime and operational tempo allow.

If your organization does not require an in-depth course on this, then adjust the needs as necessary.

Using the Lesson Topic Guide model already in use by your organization, start with an introductory lesson covering terminology, organizational standards, communication, and team concepts. Ensure that any required knowledge that must be replicated and used by all team members is discussed and trained so that the student can successfully pass a test regarding the information. More importantly, stress the need to learn the information and give examples that can motivate learning and retention.

Developing lessons that discuss and train tactics and team movement may start in the classroom but should end in practicing the tactic and explaining the movements. A learning tool here is to have the student talk the instructor through the movement explaining what they are seeing, why they are reacting to a stimulus, who they are communicating with, what they are telling the rest of the team and control, or their thought process to determine their decision to move.

Develop Testing

This course may be considered advanced training for specialized personnel, and testing should be commensurate with the needs of your organization. The testing standards of your organization should be followed for both knowledge-based and skills-based objectives.

Those conducting this training should have an expansive knowledge of dignitary protection practices and be able to communicate well, discuss the organizational standards, and maintain flexibility during sensitive and tough discussions. Therefore, the testing of those in this training may be multi-faceted, consider the following testing exercises:

- A tabletop exercise of vehicle movement and arrival and egress of a venue with supervision to assist or add stimuli.

- With the instructor acting as the protected dignitary, walk through a crowded venue while an instructor observes the protection team.

If the team is to carry weapons for the protection of the dignitary, advanced firearm training must include team tactics with a firearm, practical shooting scenarios, and possibly marksmanship from or with the addition of a vehicle.

INVESTIGATIONS

The qualities, knowledge, and skills required for a person to conduct investigations come easier for some than others. Surprisingly, some candidates do not have the ability or acuity to delve into searching for answers or qualifying statements from witnesses. Therefore, a course in investigations may be important for your organization. Many events at your organization can use the assistance of an investigator to document events that have occurred. Minor vehicle accidents, missing equipment, slips-trips-falls, safety violations, financial fraud, poor work quality, or social media-borne threats are all reasons to have a trained investigator.

Before proceeding, it is recommended that you discuss the role of an investigator with the legal department of your organization. Not that they should disagree with the role, but more importantly, how they might want issues like current and proposed laws, evidence handling, evidence collection, employee interview rights and protocols, background investigations, background investigation legal search programs, or case numbering documented. Coordination has merit.

The size of your organization and the role and production of the employees may determine the size and depth of your investigations team. Employee theft is a reality, and a robust and well-educated investigation staff can be a preventative measure.

Investigation training can also be a stairway to promotion and cross-training for your security staff. Train all staff in how to ask questions, what questions are important, legal issues when conducting a cursory investigation, and note taking and documentation of the information the staff member has uncovered. The more data gathered close to the incident, generally the easier the follow-up investigators work.

Collection, documenting, marking, and protecting evidence all require training as to your organizational protocols. Digital photography has minimized the size of evidence storage space, but unfortunately, the need for a protected space for some evidence may become critical. Evidence in a criminal case generally will be taken by law enforcement. Evidence of civil issues will be kept by your organization. Coordination with your legal team may minimize or increase some evidence storage, however since they may need to prosecute the case, they are the users of the evidence and have control of storage and length of holding.

Every correct action by an employee is trumped by another employee's misdeeds. For this reason, being professionally aggressive in pursuing answers through an investigation of events can be critical for prevention, process changes, and corrective future actions.

Co-workers who are unwilling to assist in your investigation, though they were witnesses or knew of the event are also a problem and how the organization wants those handled is a question for Human Resources and legal.

Some investigations require a level of sensitivity that may not be understood by an untrained investigator. These investigations might include workplace violence, sexual harassment, or crimes regarding the organization's cyber environment.

Misuse and potentially criminal misuse of your organization's cyber environment or assets will require advanced training and the understanding of an information technology specialist. The days of sending inappropriate emails or files across the organization's network are not over. The internet is full of users who will write ugly and harassing communications to other internet users with some anonymity. Unfortunately, such activity sometimes crosses the organizational barrier, and those same people use your internal communications to do the same. When the comments become sexual harassment, harassment, and bullying which places the organization in a position to react. Another issue for corporations is an internal user who sends copywritten materials which can jeopardize the organization's IP address and cause it to be blacklisted. In these cases, the organization's policies and user agreements need to be inclusive with Read and Understood signature pages.

An investigator is not only the person who digs for the truths and facts of an event, the investigator is also the person who must document the event and the investigation in a manner that is complete, accurate, objective, readable by most, and presented as a final and polished product with the potential of presenting this in a court of law or during a deposition.

Several professional associations offer training certificates or certifications in investigations.

- ASIS International offers the Professional Certified Investigator (PCI). Their learning objectives comprise three domains which include:
  - Ethical conflict of the case and legal regulations of the role
  - Case elements, strategies, and risks
  - Investigative goals and procedural options
  - Managing investigative resources
  - Investigative process improvements
  - Investigative techniques
  - Interviewing techniques and deceptive indicators
  - Evidence and evidence analysis
  - External information sources
  - Use of other investigative methods and technology
  - Report preparation and presentation
- The Society for Human Resource Management (SHRM) offers the Workplace Investigations Specialty Credential in which their learning objectives include:
  - When and how to engage external counsel
  - What justifies a formal investigation
  - Effective interviewing and data gathering
  - Analyzing results, and
  - Concluding and providing recommendations for resolutions.
- The Association of Certified Fraud Examiners offers the widely accepted Certified Fraud Examiner (CFE) credential. This credential's learning objectives include:
  - Knowledge of complex financial transactions
  - Understanding of investigative techniques and legal issues
  - Ability to resolve allegations of fraud
  - Design anti-fraud programs

When developing selection criteria for investigator candidates, look for proven experience conducting investigations such as former law enforcement, or other fields where interviewing and collecting information was necessary.

Define the Need

It is hard to believe that an organization has no need for a trained investigator and even an investigative team based on incidents. The need can be based on the organization's historical data. Counting the number of injuries, incidents of violence, lost or missing equipment and incidents of workplace harassment should suffice as a rationale for needing a trained investigator.

If your organizational history is full of events, there is a good possibility that senior security management is pulled away from daily duties to conduct the inquiry, some taking considerable hours that your senior staff may not have to conduct this investigation. The reality is taking a staff member away from their duties to perform an in-depth investigation may lead to a less-than-perfect investigation, evidence gathering, or comprising the report with a strategy to present the case for legal action.

A trained investigator with the sole duty of managing cases, conducting interviews, reviewing surveillance videos, collecting, cataloging, and examining evidence, will be kept quite busy. The investigator's experience will assist in streamlining case processes and ensure that only fully vetted inquiries will be forwarded for prosecution.

Another excellent benefit of a trained investigator is the view of security professionalism within your organization with the workers' compensation insurance company, local law enforcement, and possibly the courts. Submitting a poorly investigated incident can have a variety of consequences:

- The case will be dismissed due to a lack of evidence or poorly handled evidence.
- The case will require outside investigators in your facility to re-conduct the investigation.
- The case will fall to a lower status based on the amount of work required by the recipient.

Another value of an investigator may be to take over background investigations from Human Resources. Not to demean the professionals in HR, but to accept resumes, applications, and materials to conduct background investigations for those to whom a position has been offered and accepted sometimes becomes a paperwork exercise and not an investigation. An investigator will look for inconsistencies in the materials provided and query the candidate for reasons for the inconsistencies. An investigator may also review the returned background investigation to look for additional unidentified information, such as additional names used, and dates of employment that may not correspond with documentation previously provided.

NOTE:
If having an investigations arm within your department is a new endeavor for your organization, consider the necessity of newly developed policies, procedures, and associated tools for the investigators, case management, strategy, technical applications, software, and protected space for investigators to work.

Conduct a Task Analysis

Base the task analysis on your identified needs and an accounting of historical information regarding past events that led to investigations or should have been investigated. Categorize the types of incidents and a general estimate of an investigative strategy, techniques to be used during the investigation, and the hours necessary for each incident.

Consider all incidents handled by your security department and look to see if any portion of those incidents can be moved to an investigator to do follow-up interviews or take some action away from security so they can get back to their regular duties.

Addition task analysis items may include:

- The organization's existing case history and the state of evidence protection.
- Based on time, has the incident reporting system been changed causing a loss of case data?
- Over time, officers not being guided with report writing or evidence labeling can cause a problem. Having an investigator edit the evidence labeling and editing the associated report with the new labeling may be necessary.
- Are there aging cases in which evidence may not necessitate retention?

In many cases, investigators are ensuring that company policies are being followed, therefore the investigators need to know, understand, and be able to perform operations similar to the employees that they are investigating. An example is in investigations conducted by casino surveillance personnel who are overwatching a cashier in the cage, or a craps dealer. The simple truth is cross training your investigation team may be necessary.

Determine Training Form

Potentially, this courseware will have multiple training formats. Lecture for general knowledge, discussions, and organizational policies and legal issues. Tabletop exercises for planning, developing investigative strategies, and personnel assignments for large investigations. And field exercises for demonstration, practice, and certification in conducting investigations.

Develop Objectives

The policies, procedures, and other rules your organization has set for the conduct of investigations, including legal or applicable contractual issues with labor unions should be identified in the objectives. Then taking the tasks analysis and selecting the learning domain and objectives identified by professional association certificates on investigations, develop a set of objectives with specifics as to what topics are testable and how the tests will be administered.

Improperly conducting an investigation using false tactics professed in movies and television can jeopardize an organization's ability to conduct security operations and present valid evidence uncovered during the improper techniques. Or worse, false tactics may lead to the company becoming involved in a civil suit.

Depending on the types of investigations your staff will be involved with may require anywhere from an introductory class to a multi-lesson course with multiple domains.

Write the Curriculum

As discussed above, the types of investigations to be performed by your organization should determine the length and breadth of your course. For an organization that requires a more comprehensive investigation component, this course can be 40 hours with multiple additional specific courses based on the organization's operations and product offerings.

If your organization does not require an in-depth course on this, then adjust the course and topics to suit your needs as necessary.

Use the Lesson Topic Guide model already in use by your organization, starting with an introductory lesson covering terminology, organizational standards, legal concerns, and ethics for unbiased inquiries. Then moving deeper into specifics for different types of investigations, such as witness statements, and photographs, protecting the scene, ensuring the safety of responders, and caring for any injured personnel.

NOTE:
If possible, investigators do not want to be initial scene commanders, however after the scene is effectively safe, personnel have been identified and removed, then the scene belongs to the investigator. Recognizing that incidents that require investigations are a problem for normal operations, speed in collecting evidence and releasing the scene is critical to the company's interests.

Very often, after the investigation is complete, a review of photographs or video from the scene may reveal little evidentiary value. Therefore, capturing evidence with video and digital photography has several intricacies that the investigator needs to be trained in, such as placing a ruler near small items, taking photos of the scene, and including immobile objects that can be identified for placement. Photographs of an incident should never be taken with a personal phone, as the phone can then be subpoenaed. A small point-and-shoot style camera that has a flash and removable digital media is recommended. The camera should be set to document the date and time in the metadata. The investigator will need to know where the date and time will be recorded on the image, being careful so that the date and time do not cover important evidence on the photographed image itself.

Interviewing techniques can be a course within itself covering not only how to ask questions, but also how to pause and listen and look for visual clues as to the interviewee's recall or direct recall. The investigator also needs to use the correct interview technique for the situation – interviewing an employee suspected of fraud is different than interviewing a potential employee candidate.

A well-respected interview training course is the Reid technique put on by John E. Reid & Associates. They offer four-day courses for interviewing and have other courses covering specific needs such as phone interviews, sex trafficking, child abuse, military, and one for school administrators.

If your organization finds that additional training is necessary here are a few suggestions:

- How to testify in court or at deposition. To assist in your department's value, seek assistance from your legal department if an attorney with courtroom experience is on staff.
- Using Open Source Intelligence (OSINT) courses assists in identifying web assets to conduct investigations and how to use those assets.

Develop Testing

This course may be considered advanced training for specialized personnel, and testing should be commensurate with the needs of your organization. The testing standards of your organization should be followed for both knowledge-based and skills-based objectives.

Specialized Investigation Training

There always seems to be some special type of investigation that may require additional training for your staff. Unless these are common types of investigations your organization experiences, specialized training can be included in continued training events. However, they may be so specialized that sending staff members to off-site training may be seen as both a benefit for your staff as well as they can bring back what they learned and pass that information on to staff who have a similar need.

- Workplace Violence: Insurance companies may not cover injuries sustained from an unwanted act of violence.

  We are in a period where workplace violence is a nightly news item. Preparations for dealing with the aftereffects of such an event need to be in place and exercised so the organization as a whole can be ready for such an event. At the same time, policies should be drafted and communicated to all employees, customers, vendors, and any person who enters your organizational domain that any act of violence will not be tolerated and is grounds for immediate ejection from the facility, termination of contracts and termination of employment as well as the organization will seek criminal action with all prejudice.

  Remind the representatives of your organization that the harshness of the language is proof that their safety is the greatest concern of the organization. Horseplay, threats, or inappropriate touching, even as a joke, are not acceptable in the workplace. To that end, security staff must adhere to the policies that all practicing of self-defense tactics, the use of handcuffs, and any weapon are grounds for termination unless under the supervision of a supervisor or manager level determined by senior management.

- Harassment Investigation: Like the above, incidents of harassment or bullying in any form will not be tolerated. Forms can be cyber, verbal, written, or physical, and therefore the organization investigators must be able to conduct an inquiry regardless of the form. At the same time, coordinating efforts with Human Resources and legal may require the rescheduling of work schedules and even office locations.

  Events that occur after work hours may also become an issue for the organization. Threats of violence due to an employee's domestic issue may find their way into the facility. After being notified of an off-work incident or domestic issue, coordinate with legal and Human Resources to assist in protecting the employee as necessary and the organization, its facilities, and other employees.

  Employees who have been victims of various forms of harassment need to be handled with a little more care, however, the investigator and security goals are to protect the organization from a threat, regardless of the vector. If necessary, the legal department can ask for a protective order from the threat. The investigation should document all actions taken to mitigate the threat as well as collect evidence and assist legal in building a case, should the threat manifest into a reality.

- Internal Affairs Investigations: Regardless of the size of your department, security staff will be accused of improper actions, failing to perform their job, or even a crime. Internal affairs investigations regardless of what television shows tell us, do not place the investigator in a bad position. Security personnel not performing their job, treating some people differently than others, or simply acting inappropriately as identified by your policies, procedures, and the training they have received, causes other staff members to work harder or is an internal threat to the security operations.

The investigation should be conducted in an ethical and unbiased manner. As an organizational investigator who will conduct inquiries into other department personnel with improper conduct, the same issues will be found within the security staff. A common finding is that the accused employee's co-workers and peers may be unwilling to give fully truthful statements if the accusations are true and will be most helpful when the accusations are false.

Management should express to employees that their honesty is a part of their employment. And within the security department, staff that is not helpful in internal investigations may be disciplined, as this is why they were hired.

Another common finding is that the complainant cannot put into actional words the inappropriate conduct of the staff. Or the action by the security staff was not inappropriate though the complainant thought it was. In these incidents, the investigator must be personable, beyond reproach, and fully document the complaint as stated. The report is then sent to management for adjudication and response.

COMPANY SECURITY ORIENTATION/SITE ORIENTATION

This is slightly different than developing training for your security department, however, the importance of this orientation training can be seen as the basis for the security protocol of your organization. Any person who is granted badge access to the facilities, whether employees, contractors, or vendors can only be expected to act according to the security policies of the facility if they are given the knowledge of how they are expected to act in the facility, where they can access, how to use the badge or key for access and thereby be an attribute to your security operations.

The recommendation for orientation is based on a maturing process and minimization of security incidents caused by mistakes and lack of knowledge.

ORIENTATION DOCUMENTATION

Before the orientation is started, the level of access to be granted to the badge holder is received from the granting department manager of record. A protocol should exist where each department has a single point of contact or designee that is capable of identifying which level of access a new employee will be granted.

In conjunction with Human Resources, an appointment for orientation is scheduled for a set number of new hires. Using a locus of control of six new hires per orientation is based on the time it takes to make badges and conduct the orientation. A security supervisor collects data necessary for security to know and verify the identity to whom a badge is being granted as well as information regarding vehicles and emergency contact information.

All rules regarding security are listed on a single-page form that the new hire signs and acknowledges their adherence to. The form is identified as Confidential and Company Private and may not be disseminated outside of the organization. The forms are scanned and put into a security employee file maintained by security management and the paper form sent to Human Resources for their files.

The new hires then watch a video presentation that goes over the items on the acknowledged form to ensure comprehension. The importance is that the new hire has been told the same thing twice, once acknowledged by their signature and once by being given a presentation that every new hire sees.

FACILITY ORIENTATION

The new hires are given their badges and reminded of when and where they must be worn and that they should not be worn outside the organization. The badge only has a photo of the employee and their first and last name with a readily visible mark that identifies them as an employee, vendor, or customer.

During the orientation, the new hires biometrics are recorded in the system and associated with the badge. The new hires are shown how to use the badge and then use their badge and biometrics to ensure access has been granted. For new hires, a representative from the department to which they will be working walks with the new hire during the orientation tour. Customers are met by badged personnel from their company, if available.

The orientation discusses the nature of the operation, the need for a safe environment, the location of common areas, restrooms, breakrooms, and how to access their workspace, how to egress during incidents, and the need for them to be a positive attribute to the security operation.

NOTE:
The above example may be harsh and time-consuming for some operations, however after there is an incident, dealing with "I didn't know," "I wasn't aware," or "I'm sorry" is a hole in your security system. Hours are spent reacting to the incident, and possibly your security protocols are looked at unfavorably. Setting the standard from the beginning, as well as posting signage where necessary goes a long way to operational security.

Defining the Need

This effort will start with the organization's specific facility access control policies, and how badging and key management is conducted for the site. List the general rules that a new hire or any person who is being granted access to your site will need to know. Assuming your organization has been operational for some time, this should be easy to document.

NOTE:
Policies and procedures regarding physical access to your organization and its facilities are generally highly auditable by most standards. This will include the recertification of access needs, replacement of lost or stolen badges and keys, access incidents that were considered as insecurity, verification that your policies and procedures are reviewed, and substantial changes are made promptly.

Conduct a Task Analysis

Based on your identified needs and those of other departments such as Human Resources, categorize the information a person will need so they can access the facilities and areas in which they will be working and have access to information so they can become beneficial to the organization as soon as possible.

Since all new employees will receive this training, ensure the training is acceptable and agreed upon by all internal stakeholders.

Determine Training Form

As written above, the training form may have multiple formats to increase comprehension and retention. Having the new hire read the rules, watch a video of the rules than walk the site takes the passive learning options to an active learning experience and gives the candidate the chance to understand what they have just read and watched through action.

Develop Objectives

Using the policies, procedures, and other rules your organization has set for access to the facility, behavior within the facility as well as other topics such as smoking rules, parking spaces, and badge-wearing or key management should be identified in the objectives. Then take the tasks analysis and develop learning domains and identified objectives.

Write the Curriculum

Using the standardized Lesson Topic Guide structure and the objectives that were developed, document and draft the curriculum for this course.

Develop Testing

This course may not need a formal test, however, ensuring comprehension by attendees is necessary for the key points. This can be done by the employee giving the orientation who should ask questions outlined in the curriculum, looking for the correct terminology or sequence of actions.

INDEX

Note: Page numbers in *italics* refer to *figures*

Printed in the United States
by Baker & Taylor Publisher Services